SECOND EDITION

A Picture's Worth

PECS AND OTHER VISUAL COMMUNICATION STRATEGIES IN AUTISM

TOPICS IN AUTISM

SECOND EDITION

A Picture's Worth

PECS AND OTHER VISUAL COMMUNICATION STRATEGIES IN AUTISM

Andy Bondy, Ph.D. & Lori Frost, M.S., CCC-SLP

Sandra L. Harris, Ph.D., series editor

Woodbine House ◆ 2011

All rights reserved under International and Pan American Copyright Conventions.
Published in the United States of America by Woodbine House, Inc.,
6510 Bells Bell Rd., Bethesda, MD 20817. 800-843-7323. www.woodbinehouse.com

Library of Congress Cataloging-in-Publication Data

Bondy, Andy.
  A picture's worth : PECS and other visual communication strategies in autism / by
Andy Bondy and Lori Frost. -- 2nd ed.
     p. cm. -- (Topics in autism)
  Includes bibliographical references and index.
  ISBN 978-1-60613-015-5
  1. Autistic children. 2. Autistic children--Rehabilitation. 3. Interpersonal
communication. I. Frost, Lori. II. Title.
  RJ506.A9B655 2011
  618.92'85882--dc23
                                                            2011018732

Manufactured in the United States of America

10   9   8   7   6   5   4

This book is dedicated to our parents,
Jack, Char, Lily, and Harry, for all the love and support
they've provided over the years!

Table of Contents

Acknowledgements

We would like to acknowledge the contributions our families have made to making this book possible. Rayna, John, Alexis, Sam, and Joe have taught us a lot about functional communication! Their patience and cooperation throughout the extensive travel and work we've put in over the last many years has been immeasurable. Without their support and help, not a whit would have been done! We also wish to thank everyone in Pyramid Educational Consultants, Inc.—a fabulous group of dedicated international professionals and support staff who tirelessly seek to enhance the lives of the children and adults and associated family members and staff we seek to help.

Introduction

I first learned about Nate from a friend who worked in the local children's hospital. He told me that staff had worked on developing a type of body armor for this three-year-old boy, complete with helmet, elbow, wrist, and knee guards! When I asked why this boy needed so much protection, my friend answered, "Well, it's to protect him from himself." I had worked with a number of children who hurt themselves, but never one so young. He was scheduled to visit our school the next day.

Nate's mother, who appeared very caring but apprehensive, brought him to the school. She told us that he did not speak and although there were many things he liked, he almost always did them by himself. She started to talk about his "outbursts" while he was quietly sitting on her lap. Suddenly, he made a small noise and leaped out of her lap.

Instantly, Nate was on the floor, slamming his forehead onto the hard tiles. Before I could reach him, he started to run toward the door. I quickly picked him up and he immediately scratched my face and pulled my beard. While still holding him, I turned him around so his hands were further from my face. He responded by kicking backward into my stomach. I put him down, and watched as he jumped up and down on his knees. He then bolted away and smashed his face into the door. During this entire episode, which lasted no more than a minute, his mother sat quietly, looking as bewildered as all the professionals in the room.

What is the problem here? Nate was a young boy diagnosed as having autism. He was three years old but had not used speech. Were his problems with communication related to his behavioral difficulties? Were his behavioral difficulties related to his communication problems?

Were his communication difficulties only related to the absence of speech or were the issues even deeper? Finally, what strategies could Nate's mother, family members, and professionals use to best help him?

This book is intended to help parents and professionals understand the communication difficulties of children and adults such as Nate who do not speak, including those with autism spectrum disorders. This edition of the book builds on the information provided in the first edition, which was published in 2001. We have revised this book because new research has continued to provide new strategies and improved support for using these strategies to promote independent communication for children with autism and related disabilities. The problems associated with the lack or weak use of critical functional communication skills remain a significant barrier for the independent functioning of many children and adults. The recommendations in this book regarding both skills to target as well as strategies to teach those skills reflect the ever-growing body of researchers from the fields of applied behavior analysis and speech pathology.

In the early chapters of this book, we describe some of the characteristics of people who are nonspeaking, and provide examples of our approach to understanding communication. We also describe the relationship between communication and various behavioral difficulties.

In the next chapters, we describe several intervention strategies, including the use of sign language and other less formal gestural systems, and various picture- or symbol-based systems. Included in this review are a number of low-tech approaches (use of photographs and line drawings) as well as high-tech approaches (use of electronic systems, such as voice-output devices). Throughout this review, we discuss ways to assess whether an approach is appropriate for a particular child or adult.

In the last chapters, we describe various strategies using visual cues to enhance a person's understanding of our instructions, issues associated with learning to wait and deal with transitions, and how such strategies can enhance the effectiveness of different motivational strategies.

Why should we devote an entire book to helping children who have difficulty acquiring speech to communicate through other means? I think continuing with the story about Nate will help answer this question.

Nate started an intense full-time special training program organized within the public schools. First, his teachers figured out what Nate liked and what could help him pay attention to his surroundings. It was clear that while he needed to learn to imitate what people said and did, he had no such skills on entering the program.

Within a few days, Nate was taught to use the Picture Exchange Communication System (PECS). During the first training session, Nate learned to calmly give a picture of a pretzel (his favorite treat) to his teacher. This lesson was taught without using any questions from the staff—in fact, Nate was able to spontaneously give the picture to the teacher when he saw her holding the pretzel. Within a few days, he learned to use single pictures to request other favorite items.

Nate next learned to put two icons on a card to form a simple sentence. He then learned to clarify some of his requests—communicating that he wanted the BIG pretzel, for example. As he learned new ways to ask for things, he also learned to tell his teachers about simple things in the classroom. During this period of training, his parents used PECS at home to help Nate communicate with everyone in his family. Both at school and at home, Nate became much calmer and had far fewer tantrums since he now had an effective, easy system to use to let others know what he wanted.

Many people are afraid that if they introduce children to non-speech communication systems such as Nate learned to use, they will be less likely to learn to talk. We will discuss that point in more detail later, but the simple truth is that there is no evidence that visual systems interfere with or inhibit the development of speech. On the contrary, there is evidence that using such systems has a beneficial impact on speech development. As you can see, Nate learned to become an effective communicator even though he had not yet learned to speak. But the primary point of this book is **not** to emphasize strategies that will always lead to speech. Instead, this book will focus on ways to help children learn to quickly become effective communicators.

Our emphasis is on helping children to develop functional communication skills—that is, the ability to direct behavior to another person in order to receive direct rewards (such as the item they want) or social rewards (such as praise or a pleasant interaction).

The table on the next page lists the nine critical functional communication skills that are the focus of this book.

When children (and adults) acquire functional communication skills, their lives—and those of their families and teachers—become greatly enriched.

| Critical Functional Communication Skills ||
Productive (Expressive)	Responsive (Receptive)
1. Request reinforcers (desired items or activities)	1. Respond to "Wait" and "No"
2. Ask for help	2. Follow functional directions
3. Ask for a break	3. Follow a schedule
4. Respond "No" to "Do you want...?"	4. Transition
5. Respond "Yes" to "Do you want...?"	

1 | What Is Communication?

I worked with Anne from the time she was twenty-six months old. She had big blue eyes and always fixed them on me when I entered the classroom. On the day that we met, I walked over to her and picked her up. She immediately smiled, so I started to slowly spin her around while in my arms. She laughed and tossed her head back. We played this game for several minutes. The next morning when I entered the room, she ran over to me and held her arms up. I waited to see what would happen next. She used no words or even any sounds. But she continued to lift up her arms and just about walked on my shoes! Finally, her arms and pleading eyes won me over and I picked her up and spun her around. While she had not spoken, I certainly knew what she wanted!

What is the essence of communication? Is speech necessary for people to communicate? Are there ways to communicate without using speech? These are critical questions for anyone who is planning to teach communication. How we answer these questions may have important impacts on the solutions we create and try to implement.

Defining "communication" is no easy task. A Google search for "define communication" results in 37.5 million results! *Merriam-Webster Online Dictionary* (2010) defines "communication" as "a process by which information is exchanged between individuals through a common system of symbols, signs, or behavior." The American Speech-Language-Hearing Association Committee on Language defines "language" as "a complex and dynamic system of conventional symbols that is used in various modes for thought and communication." Language can be made up of spoken and written words, as the English language reasonable to assume that we must first teach a child to imitate before he can reply and before he can initiate communication, but in the next section, we will see that this may not be a universal assumption.

In terms of understanding *where* we communicate, we already noted that there must be a "listener" (or someone who responds

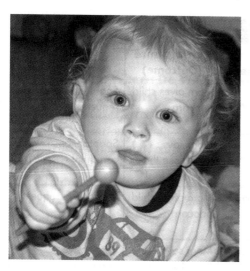

to whatever mode of communication is used) present for an episode of communication to occur. If an action, speech, or otherwise is as likely to occur when there is an audience as when a child is alone, then it is questionable whether any communication is occurring. If the child who earlier walked to the play room and retrieved a doll (without awareness that anyone else was in the room) had been muttering "doll," would that have been a communicative act? We would say "no" because no action was directed to another person.

How Do We Communicate?

Our last investigative reporter question relates to *how* we communicate. The most frequent and socially accepted way to communicate is to use speech. However, when we watch someone speaking, it quickly becomes clear that we all use facial expressions and other types of body language to enhance the effectiveness or clarity of our message. Some people feel tortured when asked to speak without using their hands! We also use various voice qualities to change the way what we are saying is understood. Such changes include our tone of voice or inflection, how loudly or rapidly we speak, or how we modulate our emphasis on certain sounds, as when using sarcasm.

Can we communicate without using speech and its various modifications? As you watch people using their hands while speaking, you can probably recognize many gestures. When those hand gestures become more formalized, we can see the roots of another communication system, sign language. In the deaf community, there are several formal sign systems, including American Sign Language (ASL) and Signing Exact English (SEE). ASL has its own set of rules for grammar, while SEE follows the rules for spoken English.

As you read this book, we are using another mode of communication, namely, writing. Although it may seem surprising, there are children who have learned to read and write but have never learned to speak. In addition to print, other symbols have been used in communication. Some written languages are picture-related, as in hieroglyphics and Chinese/Japanese, or texture related, as in Braille. Some modern systems involve a mixture of pictures and abstract symbols, as in Blissymbols or Rebus symbols. Other communication systems involve pictures or photographs, as in picture-boards, the Picture Exchange Communication System, or various electronic systems. In other chapters, we will discuss how these symbols are used. The important point here is that many types of symbols have been incorporated into sophisticated communication systems.

In short, just as Skinner specified, there are many modalities of communication used by children and adults (see Chapter 5 for more information on this topic). It is not necessary for a child to use speech in order to communicate effectively with others. On the other hand, there *are* clear benefits if a child can use speech to communicate. These advantages include its portability (I take my voice wherever I go!), the high likelihood that it will be understood, and its ease of use.

For some children with autism, their ability to understand us is far better than their ability to communicate with us. However, for many other children with autism, we will need to pay as close attention to teaching them to understand us as to teaching them to communicate. That is what we describe in the next chapter.

Refining Our Definitions

In summary, in investigating such terms as communication, language, and speech, it is apparent that in order to plan intervention for people with complex communication needs, we must further refine our definitions for optimal outcomes. We want our interventions to teach communication skills that are immediately useful in as many environments as possible. We do this by teaching what we will refer to as *"functional communication."* Using the wisdom of Skinner and drawing from our own professional experiences, we define functional communication as *behavior (defined in form by the community) directed to another person who, in turn, provides related direct or social rewards.*

References & Resources

American Speech-Language-Hearing Association. (1982). *Language* [Relevant Paper]. Available from www.asha.org/policy. DOI: 10.1044/policy.RP1982-00125.

"Communication." 2008. In *Merriam-Webster Online Dictionary.* Retrieved December 23, 2010, from http://www.merriam-webster.com/dictionary/communication.

Frost, L. and Bondy, A. (2002). *The Picture Exchange Communication System Training Manual,* 2nd ed. Newark, DE: Pyramid Educational Consultants. (A comprehensive description of implementing PECS.)

Skinner, B. F. (1957). *Verbal Behavior.* Englewood Cliffs, NJ: Prentice-Hall. (A comprehensive analysis of the key functions of communication, its acquisition, and development. Best read with other professionals.)

Sulzer-Azaroff, B. & Mayer, G.R. (1991). *Behavior Analysis for Lasting Change.* Florence, KY: Wadsworth Publishing. (Chapter on Communicative Behavior. Contains varied methods for teaching various classes of verbal or communicative behavior.)

2 | The Other Side of the Communication Coin: Understanding

Tony brought his son Ryan to the school. Tony was concerned that his son had still not developed speech even though he was now three years old. Tony also was worried that his son might be deaf. I asked him why he thought this was a possibility. Tony described how his son loved to take baths and that he took one every night. He said he would call Ryan's name and tell him it was time for his bath. If Ryan were playing in the living room, his father would say over and over, "It's time for your bath! Let's go to your bath!" Ryan would not even look up from playing with his trucks. However, if Tony turned on the faucet in the bathtub, Ryan would drop everything and run to the bathroom, taking his clothes off on the fly! Tony was confused as to why Ryan would not even blink when he shouted in his ears, but could hear the water being turned on upstairs in the other end of the house. Was hearing the same as understanding?

In Chapter One, we noted that communication involves at least two people. So far, we have focused our attention on the role of the person communicating with the second person. But how do we describe what the second person is doing? Usually, if I am speaking, you are listening. However, the word "listening" will not be broad enough to describe everything the second person might be doing because, as we have pointed out, there are other modes of communication. For example, the authors are writing and you are reading.

Both listening to speech and reading words involves *understanding*. To help children become more skilled at communication, we need not only to improve their ability to communicate but also their ability to understand when others communicate.

Just as we focused on certain behaviors to help define functional communication, so we will focus on particular behaviors to help define "understanding." That is, the only way we can know if someone understands our attempts at communication is to observe changes in what they are doing. If they don't change their actions, then we would conclude that they "didn't understand us." So, while we often think of "understanding" as something that happens within us, we must *show* that we understand by doing something different than before. Therefore, understanding is demonstrated when the communicative partner responds to the contents of someone else's communication by changing behavior in a direct (i.e., a material or specific outcome) or social (i.e., praise, encouragement, etc.) manner.

The questions we asked about *communication* also are important to ask about *understanding* communication, often referred to as *receptive language.* The first question to consider is "Why understand what others communicate?"

Why Is It Important to Understand the Communication of Others?

Just as there are two primary reasons to communicate, there are also two primary reasons to understand what someone else has communicated. For example, imagine that a girl walks into the living room and begins picking up pillows, looking under chairs as if she is searching for something. Her mother tells her, "You put your candy on the TV!" The girl smiles as she walks to the TV, picks up the candy, and begins to eat. In this case, the girl listened to her mother because understanding her mother's words led her to find the candy she wanted. As this example illustrates, sometimes we listen to what others are saying because if we understand what they say we can get the things we like (as when we are called to dinner, to go outside to play, to see a friend, etc.).

Next, imagine that a boy is playing in the living room. His father says, "Bring me the newspaper!" The boy stops what he is doing, finds the newspaper, and brings it to his father. His father immediately says, "Boy! What a great helper you are!" In this case, the boy responded to his father's words to get an item not for himself, but rather for his father. What the boy received was his father's praise and other social reinforcers. As this example illustrates, sometimes we listen to what others say because if we understand them, we obtain social attention.

There are times when a child may respond to something said for a variety of reasons. For example, if she hears her mother call her name, "Mary!" she might approach her mother because 1) sometimes her mother gives her something to eat or to play with (direct reinforcement), 2) sometimes her mother gives her hugs or starts to play a game (interactive reinforcement), and 3) sometimes her mother tells her to start a chore and later praises her for completing the task (social reinforcement). In this situation, when she hears her name called she may not perfectly anticipate what will happen next but she has had lots of experience in receiving different types of reinforcers when she responds to her mom when her name is called.

Table 2-1	Types of Receptive Communication		
Setting	**Child's reaction**	**Outcome**	**Type of communication**
Mom says, "Bring me the popcorn"	Child brings Mom the popcorn	Mom says, "Thanks"	Follow instruction to benefit someone else
Mom says, "Eat some popcorn"	Child gets popcorn	Child eats popcorn	Follow instruction for personal gain

At times, the social attention is indirectly provided. That is, there may not be any immediate reinforcement provided for responding and yet reinforcement may be on its way. For example, imagine a young girl who gets home from school. Her mother asks what happened in school that day. The girl proceeds to talk on and on about what happened with each of her friends and teachers. In this case, the girl listens to her mother's communication because it leads to additional social outcomes (that is, a longer conversation with her mother). Sometimes this type of listening occurs when there are direct questions (e.g., "What did you play with?"), while at other times we listen to indirect cues (i.e., "Boy, did I like that movie!").

When we are very young, we learn to listen because of the immediate consequences. As we mature, we learn to listen even when the consequences are delayed. For example, we listen to what our teacher says because we know there will be a test at the end of the week. We listen to the nightly news report because we may have a more informative conversation with a friend later in the day. However, whatever the time delay to the consequence, we can still distinguish differences between direct versus social benefits for having listened.

What Do We Listen To?

As young children, we learn that certain sounds are important. We hear a door opening and run to see who's there. We hear a certain tune outside and we know the ice cream truck is on our block. We hear a dog snarl and run the other way. We hear the water running into the tub, as in the example that begins this chapter, and know that it's bath time. Each sound becomes important because it is associated with particular events. We hear these sounds and anticipate what comes next.

However, listening to someone speak is different from hearing an important sound. The words used by people consist of particular sounds and sound combinations. Each language has its own sets of each. These sounds are combined into words and phrases and we must learn to understand what each combination means. That is, we are not born understanding the words of our own language. Fascinating to note is the experimental evidence that infants, shortly after birth, react differently to the sound of their mother's voice than they do to other sounds (including their mother's voice scrambled in novel ways). That is, even before formal language develops, children demonstrate different behaviors when listening to voice-related sounds versus other environmental noises. Therefore, the basic "what" we listen to in a communication framework is the vocal sounds produced by other people.

When we defined functional communication in the Introduction, we noted that it is critical that children learn to approach a communicative partner. To add to that definition, it is also important that children respond to the communicative attempts of other people. A child may learn to run outside when she hears the bell of the ice cream truck, but that involves a different type of learning than understanding when mom says, "Let's go outside and I will buy some ice cream for you." The set of sounds in the phrase "ice cream" is important only because the group in which the child communicates (i.e., those who speak English) specifically arranged for that sound-set to be associated with real ice cream. If a child grew up learning another language, say French, she would not respond the same way to the sound pattern "ice cream."

The community in which a child learns a language teaches her what specific sound-sets to listen to (rather than simply hear). For some children who have not learned to communicate or to understand, our voices are no more important than other sounds in the environment.

The "How" of Listening

When we discussed the "how" of communicating in Chapter One, we noted that there are many different modalities for successful communication. One modality involves sounds we produce when we speak. However, we also can use hand gestures and signs to effectively communicate, as well as written words, visual symbols, and various types of pictures. Furthermore, we can combine words with gestures, thus often refining or completely altering the meaning of our words.

In a similar fashion, we must learn to understand different forms of communication from other people. Not only must we learn to listen to words, but we also must learn to understand many types of visually based signals or communication. That is, we learn to understand the gestures of other people, including simple pointing, and may learn to respond to more complex actions, such as formal sign language. We learn to understand visual symbols, from traffic signs, to line drawings, to printed words. For our children to become effective at understanding communication in the broadest sense, we must arrange for them to understand many types of visual as well as auditory modalities.

It also is important to remember that even those of us who are very competent at using speech also rely on many forms of visual systems. For example, when you come to an agreement with your employer, banker, or realtor, you don't simply trust that you (or the other person) will remember the verbal agreement. You make sure there is a written (visual) contract. That is, with your boss, you make sure that there is a visual representation of all of the critical aspects of your contract to work (i.e., how much and when you will be paid, what are the benefits, how can you renegotiate, etc.).

Furthermore, most of us use some type of calendar system to help us keep track of the what, when, and where of the many things we do each week. In other words, we do not rely on our memories alone to help us recall what we are doing today, when we are supposed to go where, etc. A calendar and its entries form a visual system to help us structure the events of our lives. On a more immediate basis, we rely upon clocks and watches to help us "tell time" without trying to simply guess how long it has been since some past event. In part, we teach these skills to our children because if it is good for us, it will be good for them.

When Do We Listen or Understand Others?

When are we more likely to listen to what others have to say? Generally, the greater our motivation to obtain something, the more likely we are to listen to (or watch for) communicative signs pertaining to what we want. At the end of a long school day, for instance, a student is very likely to pay close attention to the teacher's announcement that school is over so that she can go outside and play.

On the other hand, sometimes it is other people who decide that it is time to listen. For example, if a girl is playing outside the house, she may hear her mother call her name. She's likely to now run to her and ask, "What?" Hopefully, she hears something important or interesting. Of course, some times, she merely finds out that there is one more chore to be done! In this case, when her mother calls her name, the girl is less likely to pay attention to what is said next.

There are a variety of phrases designed to get someone's attention, including, "Listen to me! Look at me! Come here! Stop what you're doing and listen! Pay attention!" The list is indeed long! If someone is too far away to hear your words, you may gesture for her to come closer, as when you wave your arms or motion for her to come. Only when she is close do you continue with your message.

Where Do We Listen?

While we take our ears everywhere, we don't always listen well in every setting. We learn to pay attention to what someone else is saying in certain places but in others, we may pay little heed to what we hear. To be successful in a classroom, a student must learn to listen for the teacher's voice above all others. Yet in the cafeteria it becomes more important to listen to what the children around you are saying.

Some children with autism act as if they are self-focused and seem not to pay attention to what is being said to them. In quiet situations, other children with autism spectrum disorders may readily attend to the only other person in the room. The goal is to teach the child to pay attention in other situations, even when other children and adults are present. To promote this type of learning, it helps to make it more rewarding for the child to listen to us—by using powerful motivators in the group situation or other settings where she does not otherwise listen to our communication.

Conclusion

In this chapter, we've focused on issues related to understanding the communication of other people. Remember that a person's use of functional communication skills may be independent of his or her ability to understand the communication from others. Some children understand what we are saying but have great difficulty learning to speak or use other modes of functional communication. Other children learn to speak but have tremendous difficulty understanding what others are saying. Some children might learn to use one modality to communicate and another one to understand others' communications. For example, one child may be able to speak but understand others best when they use visual signals. Another child may use visual communication strategies to communicate, but be able to understand what others are saying. Finally, while we all prefer that children learn to understand what is said to them, we also want them to learn to understand various visual signals so that they can become effective members of our community.

Resources

Harris, S. & Delmolino, L. (2004). *Incentives for Change: Motivating People with Autism Spectrum Disorders to Learn and Gain Independence.* Bethesda: Woodbine House.

Hodgdon, L. (1995). *Visual Strategies for Improving Communication: Practical Supports for School & Home.* Troy; QuirkRoberts Pub.
(Many helpful and practical suggestions for the use of visual aids and strategies for those with various disabilities.)

3 | Can't Talk? Can't Communicate?

I visited Catherine and her three-year-old daughter, Jill, in their home. I arrived at dinnertime and said I'd like to watch a typical meal. Catherine proceeded to make dinner while Jill banged on some pot lids. Suddenly, Jill stood up and walked to a cabinet. She did not look at her mother but instead started to pull on the cabinet door. The door didn't budge and Jill started to become more and more agitated.

Catherine quickly noticed what was happening and asked Jill, "What do you want?" Catherine opened up the door and pointed to a box of cookies and said, "This one?"

Jill continued to cry as Catherine proceeded to hold up every box she could reach. The crying was getting louder and Catherine's face was getting redder. Finally, Catherine held up one box of crackers and Jill lunged for the box. As Jill calmed down, Catherine told me how exasperated and exhausted she gets because her daughter cannot let her know which snack she wants.

Clearly, Jill has a significant problem in expressing her needs with words. By age three to four, children typically use over 1000 words, can describe things in great detail, can discuss activities and events that are not ongoing or in their immediate surroundings, and can respond to abstract questions, such as "What color is grass?" (when there is no grass in sight). In contrast, Jill is still not speaking or using gestures in a meaningful way at age three.

In fact, a delay in acquiring communication skills is one of the hallmarks of autism spectrum disorders. What is the typical sequence of speech development? In general, children begin to babble around six to nine months of age. By the sixth month, children begin to demonstrate an understanding of ways to influence their parents and other caregivers even without having clearly spoken words—through gestures, eye-contact, voice tone, and other body motions. Around the first birthday, most children have begun to use single words (and possibly some two-word combinations) and understand simple instructions such as, "Where's your nose?" and "Bring me your shoe." By their second birthday, most children can use approximately 25 to 50 words and combine them into simple sentences. They also can respond to more complex instructions, such as "Get the spoon and put it into the sink."

In contrast, the speech and communication development of children with autism and other complex communication needs is far less smooth. Some children are reported to engage in fairly typical babbling and early speech development but then show remarkable regression around their second birthday, often stopping to speak entirely. Other children with autism do not seem to direct their speech to adults or siblings. They may repeat things they hear on the radio, TV, or similar sources but not imitate what their parents or peers are saying. The often-meaningless repetition of words and phrases is called *echolalia,* a prominent feature for many children with autism who do develop speech.

As yet, we do not fully understand the causes of these two distinct patterns of speech development. However, the result is similar—children who are substantially delayed in their speech and communication development by the age of two or three, even in comparison to the development of their other skills.

Why Do Some Children Have Difficulty Developing Speech?

One of our first questions about children who do not develop speech in the typical sequence is: Is there a single cause? The simple answer is "no." A child may fail to develop speech due to a variety of factors. Some factors are related to biological issues either present at conception or occurring during gestation. Various degrees of difficulty in developing speech are associated with intellectual disability, cerebral palsy, autism, and developmental apraxia of speech (Beukelman

& Mirenda, 2005). Speech impairments also may be associated with factors that are acquired after birth such as traumatic brain injury, amyotrophic lateral sclerosis, multiple sclerosis (MS), and stroke (Beukelman & Mirenda, 2005).

In the case of autism, we do not know how the disorder is specifically related to difficulties in acquiring speech—that is, we do not yet understand what parts of the brain are influenced in such a way as to affect the development of speech. In general, there does not appear to be any distinct problem with the structural aspects of speech production (an intact tongue, lips, palate, etc.) or the motor aspects of speech production (moving the tongue, lips, jaw, etc.). Furthermore, while individual children with autism may show a history of ear infections and related temporary hearing loss, as a group, such hearing difficulties do not explain the general problems in developing speech. We also do not understand why some children with autism rapidly develop speech (including speech with unusual features such as echolalia) while other children remain mute (i.e., do not use speech to effectively communicate).

Another important question is: How prevalent is the problem? This question is not easy to answer, as the definitions describing who has difficulty developing and using speech in an effective manner has varied from study to study. Researchers indicate that approximately 1 in 100 individuals need significant assistance in acquiring effective communication strategies that do not depend on speech (Beukelman & Ansel, 1995).

Before relatively effective early intervention programs were designed, it was widely estimated that half of all children with autism remained mute (Silverman, 1996; Rutter, 1985). With aggressive early intervention, the rate of mutism drops substantially (to 15 percent or less depending upon the characteristics of the children beginning the intervention). Although there are a number of programs that have reported effective interventions, such programs have in common a strong behavioral orientation, working with well-trained professionals and parents for many hours per week over two or more years (Dawson & Osterling, 1997). To learn more about such behavioral programs, a good introduction is *Right from the Start: Behavioral Intervention for Young Children with Autism*, by Sandra L. Harris and Mary Jane Weiss (Woodbine House, 2007).

What Happens If You Can't Communicate?

In our culture, the consequences for children and adults who cannot communicate are very severe. When a person cannot communicate about those things that are most important to him, then it is up to everyone else to provide the right things at the right times. Of course, even for the most caring people, many mistakes will take place.

Inability to Communicate Wants. What happens when a young boy wants something but cannot communicate about it and, thus, does not get what he desires? All of us feel great frustration when we can't have the things we most covet. When we feel frustrated, we end up doing things that are not pleasant to others or to ourselves. Children with significant communication challenges may display aggression, tantrums, or self-injury associated with their frustration over not adequately getting what they want. (See Chapter 4.)

For example, what happens if a boy wants a cookie, but his mother gives him another kind of snack because she does not know specifically what her son wants? Even though the boy is given a snack, if it is not what he wants right now, he will feel frustrated and likely act out in some manner.

Inability to Communicate "No." How would a child react when demands keep piling up and he cannot ask for a break? In such cases, children often strike out at others or the environment as a way of forcing escape from a difficult or unwanted task. When a child cannot politely and calmly say "No thanks!" then his physical solution will appear to be a challenging behavior management issue to others. (See Chapter 4.)

Inability to Participate in Social Conversations. What about a child who communicates about fundamental needs but cannot comment or simply talk about common events during the day? Such a child may have significant difficulties in developing friendships. While we may ask our friends for special things (e.g., "Can you lend me a dollar?"), most of what happens between friends involves social interactions and consequences (e.g., "Boy, Mr. Carp is such a tough teacher!" "Wasn't that the worst movie you ever saw?" etc.). Without the ability to communicate about social events our friendships remain limited at best.

Inability to Understand Others. What happens when children do not understand what we are trying to communicate to them? For these children, the course of a day may become highly chaotic. They may not understand what is going to happen next, what they are expected to do, what they will get for doing something, where they are about to go, and with whom they are about to work. Without comprehending what others are saying (or showing, in the case of visual cues), life can be bewildering and frightening.

Children who cannot understand what others are trying to communicate to them may develop complex and lengthy rituals as a way for them to make sense of their world and establish a routine for themselves. These routines may involve self-stimulatory actions (e.g., finger flicking, rocking, etc.), routines with objects (e.g., spinning them, waving them in the air, etc.), or even verbal routines (e.g., repeating a phrase or question over and over). When such rituals are interrupted, many children become very upset and agitated. Professionals may use terms such as, "resistance to change" or "maintains sameness" to describe the pattern without focusing on the cause of the pattern. (This communicative issue is just one of several factors that may contribute to the ritualistic patterns of a child.)

At a more social level, children who have trouble understanding their peers' often-subtle social cues may appear to be awkward or socially clumsy. Children and adults with Asperger's syndrome generally have age-appropriate language, but display significant limitations in their ability to understand the social intricacies of society. For example, these individuals may have difficulty in understanding humor, sarcasm, and related slight modifications of phrases and words. They usually appear to be very literal. When someone says, "Oh, *sure!* [dripping with sarcasm] We're going outside to play" the literal child goes and puts on his coat! Tony Atwood's book (*The Complete Guide to Asperger's Syndrome,* 2008) contains numerous examples of people with Asperger's and their difficulties in understanding social complexities.

The difficulty that children with autism have communicating effectively and understanding clearly can start a difficult downward spiral. The child may avoid trying to communicate because of so many failures. This withdrawal can lead to further limiting contact with peers. Peers, in turn, may think the child is more comfortable in isolation and not push for further contact. Unfortunately, if a child with autism does not interact with peers, it virtually assures that he will not develop a more mature social style, leading to further isolation.

In short, it is not enough to monitor the academic progress of a child with autism—if he can't use his skills interacting with other people, he will not become successful in the adult world.

Who Can Benefit from Acquiring Nonspeech Communication Skills?

The short answer is that an alternate method of communication should be considered for any person who cannot:

- Use understandable words or approximations to request favorite items;
- Use words or approximations to comment about interesting things;
- Initiate, imitate, and respond to simple questions;
- Understand some of what others say, especially about retrieving simple items and following simple instructions.

These are skills that are learned by typically developing children by the time they are about one and a half years old.

If a child cannot accomplish these communicative functions via speech, then we must consider using an alternative or augmentative communication system (AAC). In general, *alternative* refers to replacements for using speech such as sign language or picture-based systems. *Augmentative* refers to enhancements of a child's current communication skills such as visual signals to help remind her about the choices there are available in a particular situation or pictures that are used to enhance speech that is difficult to understand. Such systems involve either the use of gestures and sign language or depend on various visual symbols, including pictures, photographs, icons, and/or words. See Chapter 5 for an overview.

The following are some guidelines to help you determine whether AAC could benefit your child. Parents will find it helpful to have professionals assist in collecting the necessary information and making a deliberate choice

1. Is your child effectively communicating right now?

This is the most critical question to ask! Right this very minute, can your child effectively communicate basic wants and needs to you? Perhaps he is frustrated and engaging in challenging behavior because he cannot make his needs known to you. Are you often in the position of guessing what he wants or making everything immediately available so that he wants for nothing? If your child cannot calmly and effectively communicate with you right now, there are nonspeech options that can help your child learn some very basic communication skills today.

2. How old is the child?

Children younger than eighteen months who do not effectively produce vocalizations or imitate speech might not raise professional concerns about their development. These children may show typical skills in following directions and in playing with adults and peers. They may be simply slow to develop speech while other forms of communication, including gestures, may be developing appropriately.

However, if children younger than two years are not only slow to develop speech but are also lagging in the development of social responsiveness (i.e., responding when others smile, speak, or attempt to play), imitation, and play, then significant concerns about development are appropriate. If your child is in this category, it is critically important to obtain a professional assessment from a psychologist or developmental specialist, including a speech-language pathologist capable of completing an audiology screening.

At the other end of the time scale, considerable evidence exists that children older than seven years are unlikely to develop independent speech if they haven't already done so. Yes, there are sporadic testimonials about speech acquisition in older children, but these appear to be infrequent. For older children who do not communicate through speech, focusing on the acquisition of functional communication skills via alternative modalities would be most appropriate.

3. How long has the child received quality training in vocal imitation?

When children are two years or older and do not speak, many professionals (including speech-language pathologists and behavior analysts) have promoted the development of speech via vocal imitation training protocols (e.g., Lovaas, 1987). Vocal imitation training teaches a child to repeat simple sounds (usually ones he can already make) and then moves on to imitation of sound combinations, simple words, and eventually simple phrases.

The success rate for vocal imitation programs has been very encouraging. However, there are a fair number of students who do not become good vocal imitators within three months of intense training. The estimates on this pool of children range from 10 to 30 percent. When vocal imitation training has been tried for such a period of time without success, focus should be placed on teaching functional communication skills via another modality (see Lovaas, 1987). This is not to suggest that vocal imitation training should cease. From our perspective, training should focus on functional communication skills (such as those described in subsequent chapters) that will be rapidly effective, and vocal imitation should continue to be addressed.

For many children, these two areas—functional communication and vocalization—may merge at some time in the future. (See Chapter 6 for examples of this type of outcome.)

4. How does the child currently use his vocalizations?

As Chapter One discusses, a child who is developing typically can use a particular word for one of two reasons (requesting or commenting). He can also use the word for either of these purposes in different situations (i.e., initiating vs. imitating vs. responding to questions). If your child can only *imitate* single words, he may not use spoken words for functional communication. If so, you should consider either: a) rapidly promoting nonimitative uses of spoken words, or b) introducing a nonspeech modality that promotes functional communication while addressing expansion of speech imitation and other aspects of vocalization.

For example, a two-year-old girl may imitate ten words. She may even sing a few simple songs she has heard on the television. However, when offered a favorite snack or toy, she remains silent unless someone models the exact word for the desired item. In this case, the girl is not initiating with the few spoken words she can produce. Although we would want to continue to expand this child's imitative skills, we should also address her immediate need to initiate functional communication.

In the next chapter, we will provide some information to help you understand what your child could be communicating with his behavior if he does not yet have another way of communicating. The following chapters will discuss different nonverbal communication methods that could benefit your child.

References & Resources

Atwood, T. (2008) *The Complete Guide to Asperger's Syndrome*. Philadelphia: Jessica Kingsley.

Beukelman, D. & Ansel, B. (1995). Research priorities in augmentative and alternative communication. *Augmentative and Alternative Communication, 11*, 131-34.

Beukelman, D. & Mirenda, P. (2005). *Augmentative and Alternative Communication*. Baltimore: Paul H. Brookes.

Dawson, G. & Osterling, J. (1997). Early intervention in autism. In M.J. Guralnick (Ed.), *The Effectiveness of Early Intervention* (pp. 307-326). Baltimore: Paul H. Brookes.

Harris, S. & Weiss, M.J. (2007). *Right from the Start: Behavioral Intervention for Young Children with Autism*. Bethesda: Woodbine House.

Lovaas, O.I. (1981). Teaching Developmentally Disabled Children: The Me Book. Austin, TX: Pro-Ed.

Lovaas, O.I. (1987). Behavioral treatment and normal educational and intellectual functioning in young autistic children. *Journal of Consulting and Clinical Psychology, 55,* 3-9.

Lovaas, O.I. (2002). (Ed.). Teaching Individuals with Developmental Disabilities: Basic Intervention Techniques. Austin, TX: Pro-Ed.

Rutter, M. (1985). The treatment of autistic children. Journal of Child Psychology & Psychiatry, 26, 193-214.

Silverman, F. (1995). *Communication for the Speechless*. 3rd ed. Boston: Allyn & Bacon.

4 Why Is She Doing That? The Relationship between Behavior and Communication

At a parent meeting, Sara described her current problems with her son, Adam. She knew that he enjoyed playing in the back yard. Her problem was knowing exactly when he wanted to go outside. She told the group that sometimes Adam would stand by the back door and start to scream. If no one came quickly, he would flop down and bang his head on the floor. Once that happened, Sara believed that the only thing that would calm him down was to open the door and let him go outside. Once outside, he quickly stopped crying, and Sara could go back to whatever she was doing.

As we saw in Chapter One, some behaviors are communicative, while others are not. We should add that some of the communicative actions of children, especially those with disabilities, often are not exactly what we adults would like to see! For example, Adam's way of indicating that he wanted to go outside was not a form his parents enjoyed.

A child's behavioral difficulties, including tantrums and aggression, often remain first and foremost in our minds. At the end of a long school day, we teachers are far more likely to talk emotionally to our partners about the trouble we had today (e.g., "He bit me again") rather than talk calmly about the positive things that occurred (e.g., "He took a bite of yogurt"). Understandably, the natural tendency of teachers and parents is to try to eliminate these problems immediately. However, we actually arrive at the best solutions by determining why the child is behaving as she is and then replacing that behavior with one that is more acceptable to us and yet accomplishes her goals. In this chapter we will look into the relationship between different types of behavioral problems and their link to communicative alternatives.

Which Behaviors Should We Aim to Eliminate or Reduce in Frequency?

When educators choose specific behaviors with an eye to eliminating them or reducing their frequency or severity, they refer to them as "behavior management targets." In the field of applied behavior analysis, we refer to these as "contextually inappropriate behaviors" to remind everyone that the context in which the behavior occurs is part of the problem. For example, yelling may not fit a classroom environment but is expected while watching many sports events. Hitting someone else is not tolerated within school but is exactly what is expected while boxing. So, when we want to eliminate a behavior we should consider the context as well. That is, for virtually every behavior there is a time and place in which we would consider that action to fit the situation. Trying to teach a child to never do a particular behavior would prove to be extremely difficult.

Furthermore, we need to guard against trying to change a behavior simply because we don't like it! If we want to eliminate or reduce a behavior we should be sure that it is due to one of the following reasons:
a. The behavior causes harm to the individual or someone else.
b. The behavior results in significant property damage.
c. The behavior results in significant social sanctions and thus would lead to fewer contacts with peers and others.
d. The behavior interferes with learning or completing one's job.

So, for example, if your child has a tendency to twirl her hair around her finger when she asks questions, this is not a behavior you would ordinarily try to eliminate, even though it drives you crazy. However, if your child has a tendency to pick her nose when she asks questions, you would want to eliminate the behavior because it satisfies criterion C, above. Likewise, you may be annoyed at your child's slow, side-to-side rocking motion, but if music is playing in the background, you may simply think of this as a type of dance. However, if the rocking prevents your child from completing a vocational task, you may choose to work on that behavior, since it violates criterion D.

If at least one of the conditions above is associated with a behavior, then a systematic behavior management plan should be put into place. It is beyond the scope of this book to describe the details necessary for a comprehensive plan, but one essential element involves determining how the behavior problem is functionally related to the situation, including considering whether the behavior is serving some type of communicative function. In other words, we must determine *why* the child is behaving a particular way and teach a new way (a new behavior) for the child to use to serve the same need.

For detailed information about determining the function of a behavior, you may wish to refer to *Functional Behavior Assessment for People with Autism* (2003) by Beth Glasberg.

Behavior Management Problems That Act as Communication

Some of the behaviors we target for elimination or reduction may serve particular needs of children or adults, such as helping them gain access to concrete outcomes. For example, acting a certain way may result in going outside to play, getting cookies at the check-out counter in the supermarket, getting food that someone else is eating, etc. Each of these behaviors results in access to some type of outcome.

On the other hand, some problematic behaviors result in increased attention from other people. For example, what would you do if you walked into a room and saw a very young child screaming and slapping her face? Our tendency would be to pick up the child to soothe her as quickly as possible and then to try to find out what was wrong. However, what if the child had no systematic and effective communication skills? In that case, she would not effectively communicate about the problem. Still, she may have enjoyed being picked up. What will happen the next time she sees the person who picked her up? If she is not quickly picked up, she very likely may start crying and slapping her face. From her point of view, that is what "worked" last time—crying and slapping seemed to result in getting picked up.

In such cases, the child's actions depend on a person's presence and serve a communicative function—requesting a desired outcome. It is important to note that we can identify a communicative function only if the child primarily engages in the action when someone else is present. If the child engages in the action when we are present as often as when we are absent, then we could not say that the child's action was directed toward a potential communicative partner. As discussed earlier, the essence of communication involves behavior directed toward another person.

Other actions of children and adults may serve a different communicative function—namely, escape or avoidance. For example, when given a difficult task, a child may begin to scream and hit herself.

I met Lisa while visiting a school for teenagers with severe cognitive limitations. At the time, Lisa was sixteen years old and had no speech or other formal communication system. I had been asked to observe her because she was reportedly becoming increasingly aggressive and self-injurious.

I observed Lisa sitting in her classroom. A teacher approached and said, "Lisa, it's time to work." The teacher showed Lisa a box filled with vocational materials. Lisa immediately began screaming while forcefully punching her thighs with her fist and biting the back of her other hand. The teacher calmly walked away with the box. Twenty minutes later, the teacher returned with another box of materials and the same message. Again, Lisa screamed and hurt herself. The teacher removed herself and the materials. After another twenty minutes, the teacher returned, issued her direction, and showed Lisa a box containing a comb and brush. Lisa calmly took the comb and brush and started brushing her hair. Lisa was a very effective communicator!

In trying to understand Lisa's actions, several factors are important to consider. First, when Lisa was left alone, she sat quietly and did not engage in screaming or self-injury. Next, she did not begin the tantrum until she looked at the materials that her teacher offered. When she liked the materials and associated activity (i.e., the hairbrush), she calmly proceeded with the activity. When she did not like what she saw, then she screamed and hit herself (and the teacher if she approached). The teacher then removed the materials and Lisa gradually calmed down. Her action was communicative because it occurred when the teacher approached and it served as an effective way to have her teacher remove the unwanted items. That is, Lisa avoided working on activities she didn't like because her teacher would remove things after Lisa started the tantrum. If Lisa had formal functional communication skills, she would have communicated that she did not want to do certain tasks (e.g., "I don't like that job"; "No thanks!" etc.). Then her teacher could have discussed why it was an important activity or offered a better incentive for Lisa.

In addition to learning how to use behavior to avoid certain activities, many children and adults learn how to escape from some activities. These activities may be:

1. difficult,
2. boring,
3. too long in duration,
4. associated with too little positive feedback (as in, "Hey, the pay around here is terrible!"),
5. in environments that are too noisy, crowded, chaotic, cold/hot, etc.

As an adult, it is likely that you have had to work (or study) in situations or environments in which one of these factors was in effect. Most adults, however, have learned certain communicative skills that may help in such circumstances. Instead of simply screaming and running away (which we have all considered!), we may ask for a break—some time away from the job. We could also communicate about issues that may help improve the work situation—such as asking for help, asking for more supervision, increasing the number of scheduled breaks each day, opening a window, etc.

Behavior Management Problems That Are Not Communicative

So far, we have reviewed that certain behaviors may serve a communicative function related to:

1. obtaining a reinforcing outcome,
2. escaping from or avoiding a person, item, or activity.

However, not every behavior management target serves one of these communicative functions. Remember, as Chapter One discusses, not all behaviors are communicative. Sometimes, we simply act on the world without any communicative involvement of another person. Furthermore, sometimes we do things that are not viewed as purposeful or rational. That is, some of our actions are best viewed as emotional reactions to the circumstances at hand.

One day, I (AB) walked into the empty lobby of a large office build-ing, intending to visit the state office on the thirty-fifth floor. I had visited this office many times over the past few years. As in the past, I calmly pushed the elevator button. On this day, however, nothing happened. I stood for a moment and noticed that the elevator had not arrived. I pushed the button again. Still no response. Now I pushed the button in several quick, hard bursts. Still nothing happened. I began pounding on the button with great effort. I also noticed, without a sense of pride, that I was muttering a series of unspeakable curses. Suddenly, my boss approached. I stopped cursing and pounding and calmly said that the elevator seemed to be out of service.

We imagine that each of you has had a similar experience. Clearly, the type of behavior is not communicative. Although I did say a few choice words, they were not meant to be heard by anyone else, as demonstrated by my change in behavior when I saw my boss. Was this behavior rational and learned from experience? No. Not only does pounding on the button rarely work, this type of reaction occurs the first time we encounter a recalcitrant piece of machinery. Furthermore, I don't recall any lessons from my mother in which she said, "Now, here is what to do if the elevator gets stuck...." The question remains, why do we have this type of explosive reaction or outburst?

For me, getting to the thirty-fifth floor was important because it was the only way to get to my job, which meant it was the way to get my pay (no work, no pay). When you and I, and our children, encounter situations in which we expect to get a rewarding outcome, and that outcome is delayed or removed, we react in this emotional manner.

One other circumstance that may elicit similar emotional reac-tions is being in pain. Studies with laboratory animals have indicated that if an animal is paired with another animal and is given unavoid-able pain (via electric shock), then the animal that is shocked is very likely to become aggressive to its companion. This aggression does not help reduce the rate of the shock but it is still a reliable outcome to this circumstance. Other research has indicated that if an animal is alone, and receives unavoidable shock, it may begin to injure itself. For obvious reasons, such work has not been done on children (with or without disabilities). However, Ray Romanczyk (Romanczyk & Mat-thews, 1998) has collected data regarding some children who forcefully hit their own heads, demonstrating that when they were in pain (as measured by pressure on their eardrum during an infection) they were much more likely to hit themselves than when they were not in pain.

In short, there can be many possible explanations for any given behavior we observe. Some may involve communication, such as when a girl hits her head to indicate that she does not like something or wants attention or to leave the area. However, that same behavior may also occur without any communicative intent when reacting to the loss of an expected reward, or to pain. How we explain the head-hitting will influence the type of intervention we design for the girl. If we decide her actions are communicative, we can use some of the techniques described in Chapters 5, 6, and 7 to teach her a better way to communicate. If we decide her actions are noncommunicative, we can use strategies in Chapter 8 to help her better handle her frustrations.

What Is Functional Communication Training?

One reason we emphasize the *why* associated with a behavior and not just its form (the *how*) is because we assume that there are several ways to achieve the same goal. That is, if a child is trying to gain attention, then we will assume that there are many different actions that she could use to achieve the same outcome—gaining attention. If this is a safe assumption, then our plan may be to teach the child another way to gain attention—one that does not involve self-injury or other disruptive actions.

An area of study called *functional communication training (FCT)* is devoted to investigating this general strategy of determining the reasons underlying behavior and then teaching different ways to achieve the desired outcome. In one of the first studies of FCT (Carr and Durand, 1985), two researchers worked with children displaying aggression or self-injury. They found two distinct reasons for these behaviors. Some children seemed to act out when they were given work that was very difficult. Their problematic behaviors appeared to communicate their need for help. A second set of children seemed to become upset if the teacher was not paying attention to them, whether the lesson was easy or difficult. Their problematic behaviors appeared to communicate their need for encouraging feedback from the teacher. The question was, what should each group of children be taught?

The children who appeared to need help were taught to request help using a simple phrase. Once they communicated this request, help was provided. After learning this skill, these children showed clear improvements in their difficult behaviors. The other children were taught to say, "How am I doing?" When staff heard this question, they immediately praised the child for working on the lesson. Again, once this skill was learned, significant improvements were noticed. Interestingly, these researchers also studied what would happen if a child were taught the skill that did not fit his or her problem. That is, children who needed help with a difficult task were taught to say, "How am I doing?" Staff would respond to this statement but not the child's need for help (since the child did not ask for help). Learning statements that did not result in the needed outcome did not help the children behave more appropriately.

Therefore, if we are to teach a new communication skill to replace a problematic behavior that the child uses as a communication strategy, then we must be certain that the new skill accomplishes exactly what the child was trying to accomplish. That is, children who need help must be taught to ask for help, while those needing more feedback need to learn to request feedback. Similarly, children who need to take a break from a boring or difficult activity must learn to request a break. The function of the new skill must match the function of the old behavior management target. Research has suggested that it should not take the child any more effort to use the new skill than it does to perform the action being replaced (Frea & Vittemberg, 2000).

How Do We Determine the Functional Control of a Behavior?

There are several strategies to help us figure out why someone is engaging in a particular behavior. (This is referred to as the *functional control* of the behavior by behavior analysts.) In general, the idea is to identify the *antecedents* of the behavior (i.e., what occurs before it), as well as the *consequences* (i.e., what the child gets out of the behavior).

A functional *assessment* can be conducted by interviewing teachers, parents, and other helpers in a systematic fashion using a structured checklist (Charlop-Christy & Kelso, 1997). A more intense form of assessment can be conducted by carefully collecting data regarding the relationship between the behavior and various factors, including

1. time of day
2. activity

3. people present
4. length of activity
5. presence of demands (including a high rate of instructions, new instructions, etc.)
6. removing or denying access to reinforcing items

Knowledgeable staff can add other factors. Once sufficient occurrences of the problem behavior have been observed, it is possible to correlate the potential factors with the likelihood of the behavior occurring. While such correlations do not prove the relationship, they can help point out factors that are most likely to be contributing to your child's problem behavior.

The most precise information on the causes of behavior can be collected via a formal *functional analysis*. In this type of study, staff trained in behavior analysis make specific environmental modifications (i.e., adding demands, ignoring the behavior, providing a stimulating environment vs. a boring environment) and then monitor corresponding changes in the child's target behavior. While this procedure yields the most accurate information about the potential causes of the behavior in question, it also is quite demanding.

Under the Individuals with Disabilities Education Act (IDEA) your child's school must agree to conduct a functional behavior analysis if: 1) she has behaviors that are interfering with her learning at school, and 2) if she is receiving special education services. Parents can arrange for a behavior analyst to conduct this assessment, but a school team can choose to develop a plan independent of recommendations from the parent's consultant.

When Is the Best Time to Teach Alternative Communication Skills?

After you have recognized that your child is having a behavior problem related to difficulty in communicating, and have determined what her behavior is communicating, you should look for opportunities to teach her an alternate way to communicate to achieve the same outcome. As the story below illustrates, not every moment is a "teaching moment" for children with autism.

I watched Amanda playing with several toys. She picked up one piece and tried to fit it into another piece. She pushed and pushed but the parts would not fit. She began to rock, then whimper, and then scream. She threw down the piece and then scattered every piece within reach. She was now in the midst of a full-blown tantrum! I walked over to Amanda and calmly said, "You need to ask for help!" Amanda whimpered, "Help!" I guided her to connect the pieces and she continued to play quietly. However, I reminded myself that Amanda and I had gone through this same sequence yesterday, and the day before that, and the day before that, and ….

Early in my career (*AB*), I used this strategy and watched many other people using similar tactics. We would observe a child's problem and then encourage her to "use her language" to solve the problem. However, I found that when I used this strategy, the child continued to have tantrums in difficult situations, and only asked for help when I reminded her. It took me many years to figure out that the child had learned precisely what I had taught. From her perspective: a) If you have a broken toy, start screaming, then … b) Andy will come over and tell you to say something, then … c) Say what Andy wants and he will help you.

The reason that Amanda was not learning to request help was that I was not teaching her to recognize the situation as one in which she should spontaneously request help. I had taught her that I would recognize that she needed help (by watching her have a tantrum) and then would remind her to use her words. I realized that if I wanted to teach Amanda to ask for help, I must teach her to ask for help before she has the tantrum. That is, when I am watching Amanda having a tantrum, I must prepare to start a lesson after the tantrum has ended.

In general, teaching any new skill in the midst of a tantrum or other type of emotional display is very difficult. A better long-term solution is to recreate the problem situation and guide the child through an effective alternative. In this way, we are striving to prevent tantrums from starting rather than emphasizing how to eliminate them once begun. Just as it took me years to learn how to effectively teach this lesson, most children require many opportunities to acquire a skill. A teacher must have patience to know that there will be more opportunities in the future, and need not teach a lesson that will make the child more dependent. Teachers must create situations in which the child becomes more independent in her use of spontaneous communication.

In our example with Amanda, a more effective strategy would be to first give her a toy that didn't work as she expected. As soon as she noticed the problem, and before she started the tantrum, she would be helped to communicate, "Help!" (See next section.)

How to Begin Teaching a Child to Communicate "Help!"

Materials needed:
A favorite toy that you have sabotaged so that it doesn't work.

Teachers needed:
One teacher to create the problem situation;
Another teacher to manually assist the child

Background:
Harry, who does not speak and is just learning to communicate, likes to play with a motorized fire truck that has a flashing light and a siren. His mother, Lily, has observed that if the fire truck isn't working properly (i.e., the battery has run down, the wheels get stuck, the siren doesn't sound, etc.) then Harry throws down the truck, screams, and starts to fiercely slap his head. When Lily has seen this happen, she has quickly fixed the truck to stop Harry from hurting himself.

Teaching scenario:
Lily has asked her daughter, Doris, to help teach Harry to calmly request help. Lily asks Doris to sit behind him. When Harry isn't looking, Lily takes the battery out of the fire truck and then hands the truck to Harry. He quickly takes it and turns on the switch to make the siren sound and the lights flash. Nothing happens!

At the earliest signs of agitation, Doris quickly helps Harry pick up the truck and give it to Lily. Lily immediately says, "Oh, you need help!" while giving Harry the battery and helping him put it into the truck. Harry then tries the switch again and is very happy that the truck now works.

During the next few days, Lily and Doris repeat this lesson with Doris gradually reducing her assistance. By the end of the week, when the truck doesn't work, Harry picks up the truck on his own and gives it to his mother. His mother and Doris switch roles so that Harry quickly learns to ask for help from whoever is nearby. Over time, his mother creates new problems for Harry to solve with his new skill, including a container that won't open, a juice box without a straw in it, and a small radio that isn't working.

Long-term strategies:

This initial strategy—giving your child things that don't work right—is similar to what everyone observes typically developing children do at a very young age. Just as these children learn to refine their ability to ask for help over time, so, too, will Harry learn to adjust his skills. For example, he may learn to use a "help" symbol within a visual communication system. The strategies to teach him how to use such a symbol will be the same as described in Chapter 6. The benefit of using two teachers for the initial aspects of this lesson will hold true whether Harry uses visual symbols, sign (formal or informal), or speech.

Conclusion

In this chapter, we've reviewed many types of behavioral difficulties your child may display. The best solutions will involve:

1. Determining what is causing the behavior,
2. If the behavior is communicative, what is your child trying to communicate?
3. Determining a good alternative communicative behavior.
4. Determining if your child can already use this alternative. If not, teach your child the new communicative alternative behavior.
5. Creating many opportunities for your child to use this new alternative.

In our next chapter we will review several communication modality options. After that, we will focus on using one of those methods (PECS) with children with autism.

References & Resources

Carr, E. G. & Durand, V. M. (1985). Reducing behavior problems through functional communication training. *Journal of Applied Behavior Analysis, 18,* 111-26.

Frea, W.D. & Vittemberg, G.L (2000). Behavioral interventions for children with autism. In J. Austin & J.E. Carr (Eds). *Handbook of Applied Behavior Analysis.* (pp. 247-73). Reno, NV: Context Press.

Glasberg, B. (2003). *Functional Behavior Assessment for People with Autism: Making Sense of Seemingly Senseless Behavior.* Bethesda, MD: Woodbine House.

Koegel, R. & Koegel, L. (1996). *Teaching Children with Autism: Strategies for Initiating Positive Interactions and Improving Learning Opportunities.* Baltimore: Paul H. Brookes Publishing Co. (A reader-friendly book describing ways to promote the development of many useful skills with children with autism.)

Romanczyk, R.G. & Matthews, A. (1998). Physiological state as antecedent: Utilization in functional analysis. In J.K. Luiselli & M.J. Cameron (Eds.), *Antecedent Control Procedures for the Behavioral Support of Persons with Developmental Disabilities.* New York, NY: Paul H. Brookes.

5 | Augmentative and Alternative Communication Systems

by Pat Mirenda, Ph.D. and Brenda Fossett, Ph.D.

Pamela is a ten-year-old girl who has autism and limited speech. Despite this, she is a successful communicator both at school and at home. When she wants something within her visual range, she leads a family member, classmate, or teacher to it and vocalizes. When she wants something that is out of sight or in another location, she points to line drawing symbols in a communication book. Pamela also uses line drawing symbols for her daily schedule and as a component of her reading curriculum. During recess and lunchtime, she and her friends enjoy looking through her communication book, in which there are pictures of Pam, her family, and her friends doing fun activities (like trick or treating on Halloween!).

During writing or math activities in her classroom, Pamela uses a computer to write, because she has difficulty manipulating a pencil and paper. She also uses a computer at home to play games with her sister and her dad. Last but certainly not least, Pam uses her limited speech to greet people, ask for help, and say "no!" when she doesn't like what is happening.

Pamela is a very fortunate child! It is clear that she has been supported by family members and school personnel who understand that her lack of speech doesn't mean she has nothing to say, and who have made systematic efforts to provide her with an individualized augmentative and alternative communication (AAC) system. Just like you and I, Pamela communicates in a variety of ways, depending on the situation. One AAC technique will *never* meet all of a child's communication needs, so a combination of approaches will be needed. This is important to remember when supporting children with autism who are just beginning to learn about communication. In this chapter, the combination of all of the symbols and devices used by a child is referred to as his or her AAC *system*.

What Is AAC?

The term augmentative and alternative communication (AAC) refers to interventions designed to compensate for the expressive communication impairments of individuals. The word *augmentative* suggests that these interventions can be used to improve upon the effectiveness of communication through existing means (including speech), while *alternative* implies developing systems that temporarily or permanently replace speech.

A host of modalities can be used to augment or replace speech, including:

- residual speech,
- vocalizations,
- pictures or related visual symbols (from photographs to print),
- Braille,
- gestures (informal or within a formal system such as American Sign Language), or
- various switch-activated devices (operated by any body action, including eye gaze).

Each of these modalities is explored in detail below.

Under the Individuals with Disabilities Education Act (IDEA), AAC systems are considered a type of "assistive technology." The 2004 amendment to IDEA assures the right of every child to have an assessment regarding the need for assistive technology. When children are determined to need assistive technology, including AAC, the public school has an obligation to provide the necessary devices or adaptations (and the training to support staff in its use) at no cost to the child's family. Parents or teachers who believe a child may need such assistance should insist that an AAC specialist consult with the child's educational team.

For more information about the field of AAC in general, the International Society for Augmentative and Alternative Communication (ISAAC) has provided useful information to professionals and lay people for almost 20 years. (See contact information at the end of this chapter.)

Why Use AAC?

AAC techniques can reduce the frustration experienced by many children with autism who do not speak. As you read in Chapter 3, teaching communication alternatives is one way to reduce or prevent behavior problems that stem from frustration. For example, AAC techniques can be used to teach children to ask for what they want, ask for help, or ask for a break from an activity instead of having a tantrum, screaming, or engaging in other problem behaviors. Children can be taught to use manual signs, photographs, line drawings, or other symbols for this purpose. When a child learns to communicate via any modality, he then will be able to better participate in play and other school activities, and is more likely to be perceived in a positive light by peers.

What about Speech Development?

One of the most common concerns expressed by parents and teachers regarding the use of AAC techniques with children with autism is how it is likely to affect speech development. The good news is that there is ample evidence that AAC techniques do *not* interfere with the development of speech—in fact, AAC may *promote* speech development in some children. For example, in Chapter 6 you will read about the Picture Exchange Communication System (PECS), an instructional approach for teaching children how to use symbols to communicate. You will also read about some of the outcome data from PECS that suggests that many children who initially learn to communicate in this way develop speech over time. It appears that once children have learned to use 30 to 100 symbols to communicate using PECS, they often begin to speak. Many are eventually able to use only speech for communication and discontinue the use of PECS altogether.

A number of studies have investigated the effect of AAC on speech production in children with autism. Recently, a group of researchers reviewed six studies where AAC intervention involved the use of manual signs (Millar, Light, and Schlosser, 2006). Of the 72 children exposed to manual signs, none showed a decrease in speech production. Children who improved in speech production tended to be those who had good verbal imitation skills.

These researchers also reviewed ten studies where AAC intervention involved the use of "low tech" AAC systems, such as PECS. All of the 167 children involved in the studies reviewed showed improvements in either verbal approximations or speech production. Finally, the same authors reviewed two studies where the AAC intervention involved the use of speech generating devices (i.e., computerized devices where an individual presses one or more buttons and a message is "spoken" by the computer). All nine of the children involved demonstrated improvements in speech production. In 2009, one of the authors of this review (Millar) updated it with additional studies that involved individuals with autism. These studies also showed that AAC does not appear to interfere with speech development, and, for some individuals, can support speech production.

When considering the potential problems that can develop when children with autism do not have a means to communicate (e.g., problem behavior, loss of learning and social opportunities, etc.), it is clear that a "wait and see" approach to AAC intervention can be detrimental. Based on current information, it is better to introduce AAC early. Some children may develop sufficient speech and no longer require AAC, many may continue to use AAC along with speech, while a few may continue to use AAC entirely. Withholding AAC intervention while waiting for the possibility of speech to develop may result in the child developing additional problems such as challenging behavior. Instead, it makes more sense to provide AAC early. This will help the child to communicate with greater ease, thereby reducing frustration.

Types of AAC Symbols

Communicating without speech requires the use of alternative symbols. A symbol is something that stands for something else. There are two main types of AAC symbols: unaided and aided. Unaided symbols do not require any equipment to produce, and include gestures, body language, vocalizations, and manual signs (among others). Aided symbols require devices that are external to the individuals who use them, such as communication books, voice output communication devices, and computers. In the next section, we will review the most commonly used AAC symbols (both unaided and aided) and discuss some of the primary advantages and disadvantages of each.

Unaided Symbols

Natural Gestures and Body Language

Before children learn to use speech, they engage in a wide array of communicative gestures. Some of these gestures appear to be natural extensions of other actions. For example, pointing is very similar in form to reaching for something. Others seem to develop as an extension or a pantomime of actions. For example, if a basketball player is about to shoot a foul shot in a basketball game and sees an opponent holding his hands around his own neck, he may tell himself not to "choke." Still other gestures are more formal, and, like spoken words, have meanings only within a given culture. For example, in North America, most people know that the "V" sign made with the fingers means either "victory" or "peace" (depending on the age of the person making the gesture)!

Although many gestures involve hand motions, we also use other parts of our bodies to convey messages. we can shrug our shoulders in doubt, frown in puzzlement, or hold out our hands and arms to ask for assistance. Perhaps the most familiar gesture involves nodding and shaking the head to mean, "yes" or "no."

People use gestures to communicate many types of messages. Perhaps the most obvious is communication about wants and needs. For example, we may hold out two toys to a child, say, "Which one do you want to play with?", and expect the child to point to or simply take the desired toy. Similarly, before they are two years old, typical children learn that they can get help from adults by simply bringing objects to them. They also learn that they can get people to look at objects or events of interest by pointing to them. Other gestures, such as waving hi or bye, blowing a kiss, and playing peek-a-boo, are used for purely social reasons. Still, they are extremely important in developing smooth social interactions between friends or between children and adults.

Why are gestures important? A common mistake in teaching communication skills to children with autism is neglecting to incorporate natural gestures as components of a communication system. This mistake often occurs because many parents and teachers tend to view communication as an "either-or" skill: either the child communicates this way *or* the child communicates that way—which, of course, is not the case! Because these children have so much difficulty learning what communication is all about, it is important to respond to and encourage them to use *all* forms of communication, as long as those forms are understandable and socially acceptable. For example, when Joshua leads his father to the cupboard to ask for a treat, or when Juanita cries after she falls down and skins her knee, they are communicating messages ("I want something" and "Ow! That hurt!") that should be respected and acknowledged.

How can gestural use be encouraged? Children with autism are likely to benefit from playful interactions that encourage them to use gestures to communicate. An example is the "Row, row, row your boat" game that Joshua's dad plays with him every evening before bedtime. Josh and his father sit on the floor facing each other with their feet touching, and they hold hands. While Josh's dad chants the "Row, row, row your boat" song, they rock back and forth to the tune. Every few lines, Josh's dad pauses in the song and waits for Josh to pull on his hands or make a noise before he continues. When they first started playing this game, Josh didn't know what to do, and would often just sit there when his dad paused. But little by little, Josh started to use body language and vocalizations during the pauses, and his dad responded right away by continuing the game. By responding to Josh's behaviors, his dad did a great job of teaching Josh to ask for "more!" Soon, Josh began to pull on people's hands and to vocalize in other situations as well, when he wanted "more."

This playful orientation can be adapted to other situations. For example, if your child likes to be picked up and spun around, you could first spin him around, then put him down and wait for him to raise his hands to indicate he wants to be picked up again. Initially, you might have to raise his arms for him, saying something like, "You want to go up again?" Little by little, you would withdraw your physical assistance until he was reaching his arms up to you himself. These examples show how easy it is to practice using gestures in the context of playful interactions and routines.

How can gestures be taught directly? It is likely that typical children learn to use gestures for communication by imitating the gestures made by adults and other children. Most children with autism have difficulty learning to communicate through gestures, at least in part because of their known difficulty with imitation (Stone, Ousley, & Littleford, 1997; Stone, Ousley, Yoder, Hogan, & Hepburn, 1997). Thus, how we teach a child with autism to use gestures will largely depend on other skills he displays.

If your child *can* imitate head and hand actions, then demonstrating various gestures and their meanings will be quite helpful in teaching. On the other hand, if he *cannot* imitate, demonstrating gestures is not likely to be successful. In such cases, teaching him to imitate will be important for the acquisition of many skills, including the use of gestures. However, while you teach imitation, you can also help your child acquire useful gestures by physically assisting him to make the motions required.

The key to using physical assistance to teach gestures is creating situations in which the gestures will prove important to your child. If gestures are not taught within situations where they are typically used and truly important, it is unlikely your child will learn to use them spontaneously. For example, consider the gesture, "waving hello." It is clear that there are several types of situations in which this is an appropriate action. If Dad enters a room and waves hello to Mark, then it would be appropriate for Mark to wave back. In addition, when Mark walks into a room, even if Dad doesn't wave hello, it would be appropriate for Mark to initiate and wave hello to him. Such natural situations would be excellent times for someone who acts as the "teacher" (such as Mom or another adult) to physically prompt Mark to wave "hello."

Physical prompts may start out fully hand-over-hand, but may be *faded* (i.e., reduced in strength) gradually in intensity and type over a series of opportunities. In general, the more important the outcome is to your child, the more likely it is that he will tolerate physical prompting. Over time, the positive and enthusiastic reaction he gets from dad is likely to result in him learning to use this gesture as a greeting.

For additional information on teaching children with autism to imitate social gestures, you may want to read *Reaching Out, Joining In: Teaching Social Skills to Young Children with Autism* by Mary Jane Weiss and Sandra L. Harris (Woodbine House, 2001).

What about teaching children to understand gestures? It is important to teach children to understand gestures as well as to use them. Otherwise, it is difficult to communicate messages efficiently and rapidly in many situations. For example, one important gesture for a child to understand is what we mean when we point to something. Usually, we at least want the child to look at what we are pointing to. Sometimes, we also want the child to retrieve an item that is pointed out ("Get that"), to put something in the direction we point ("Put it there"), or to remain in the place we point to ("Wait right here"). We usually accompany pointing with verbal directions to clarify the exact message—but the pointing itself is a critical part of the interaction. Similarly, gestures that involve social routines, such as waving goodbye, giving a "high five," or clapping to show approval, are important for the child to understand if communication is to be effective and efficient.

To teach your child to understand gestures, you first must be certain that the gesture you are teaching is truly important to him. For example, let's go back to the "pointing" example and consider Harry's situation. Harry likes to complete puzzles and thus enjoys getting each puzzle piece to complete the task. His mom decides to put all of the puzzle pieces in a box except for the first few, to provide a motivating context for teaching Harry to understand what she means when she points. When Harry begins to look for the next puzzle piece, she points to the box and then immediately taps it with her finger. Harry looks at the box when he hears the tap, lifts the lid, and takes a puzzle piece. Over the next several trials, instead of immediately tapping after pointing, mom gradually increases the delay between the two actions. Over time, Harry learns to respond to mom's pointing as a signal to get the next piece. This time-delay technique can be adapted to teach children to understand other types of gestures as well.

Manual Signs

You are probably familiar with the language systems of manual signs used by people who are deaf. Some individuals who are able to hear but have difficulty understanding and/or producing speech—such as children with autism—may also use manual signs. There are several different systems in which people use movements by their fingers and hands (augmented by other body actions) that represent letters, words, or phrases.

Manual signs can be used for both expressing and understanding language. Manual sign *input* occurs when people communicate with the child using signs to augment their speech. For example, Felicia's teacher speaks at the same time she signs the key words in her message. So, when it is time to do math, she tells Felicia, "Get out your book and a pencil" while signing *get, book,* and *pencil.* She does this because Felicia seems to pay attention more readily and follow directions more accurately if she is provided with signed information in addition to speech. To be sure, some children only *seem* to listen better when sign is added to speech, when in fact they are only relying on the visual cues. For each child, it is important to try to determine whether combining modes of input actually helps.

Manual sign *output* occurs when the child with autism uses manual signs to communicate to others. For example, when Matt wants to use the family computer at home, he asks his mom to turn it on by signing, *"want computer."*

Manual signing used to be the most commonly used system of communication for people with autism who do not use speech. One reason is that manual signs are totally "portable" and require no external devices to use. However, many people with autism seem to find it easier to use AAC systems that use symbols that are more concrete and permanent than manual signs. For instance, visual-spatial communication symbols such as pictures or line drawings work better for many children with autism. Furthermore, most parents, teachers, and classmates do not understand manual signs, and some children with autism do not have the manual skills (whether fine motor or finger dexterity) that are needed to produce them.

Decisions about whether or not to teach children to use manual signs for output are complicated and should be made by the team of people providing educational supports to your child. Factors to be considered include:

- whether your child can learn signs via imitation or physical prompting,
- your child's degree of motor skill,
- how rapidly he can acquire vocabulary in sign language vs. in other modalities,
- the portability of the system (you can take your hands with you everywhere!) compared to other systems being considered,
- and the likelihood that the signs will be understood by significant others (at school, home, and in the community).

Aided Symbols

Real Objects

The easiest type of aided symbol for most people to learn is a *real object symbol*, a three-dimensional object (or partial object) that stands for an activity, place, or thing. For example, Maria uses real object symbols to ask for what she wants and to share information with others. If she's thirsty, she brings her teacher a cup to ask for something to drink. If she wants to go out in the car, she brings her mom the car keys. After she goes to the park, she can tell her sister what she did by showing her the Frisbee that she enjoys using there.

For Maria, the cup, keys, and Frisbee are symbols representing "I'm thirsty," " I want to go out in the car," and "I went to the park." These specific symbols were selected for Maria because she always drinks from a cup, sees her mom use those keys, and carries the Frisbee to the park. She has learned from experience to associate the symbols with the activities they represent. Limitations of using such objects include their limited portability (which may be improved by use of miniatures) and the risk that they will be unavailable when needed.

Photographs

Photographs are more difficult to learn to use than real object symbols because of their greater symbolic relation to those objects, but can still be very useful. As part of an AAC system, photos may be used to represent specific people, places, activities, or items. For example, Hoa uses photos of food items to ask for her lunch in the high school cafeteria. She can talk to her classmates about her family by using photos of them, and can tell her teachers that she went to San Diego for her holiday by showing postcards and photos of the places she visited.

The advantage of photographs is that they are easier to carry around than are real object symbols. The disadvantage is that they have to be taken with a camera, bought, downloaded from the Internet, or cut out of magazines or other media, so they can be time-consuming to produce. Fortunately, digital cameras are now available to most of us. These cameras permit computer files of pictures to be stored and modified, using various software programs. Useful photographs can then be readily copied and shared, while those that are not used frequently can simply be deleted. The cost of color printing is now fairly reasonable and may permit colored symbols (both photographic and drawings). However, while color may enhance some children's ability to use a symbol, this is not the case for all children. That is, some children may respond very well to black-and-white photographs (or drawings) early in training.

Line Drawing Symbols

Line drawings may be black and white or color illustrations of objects meant to represent people, places, activities, and items, as well as actions (eat, sit, sleep, etc.), feelings (happy, angry, bored, etc.), descriptors (hot, little, up/down, etc.), and social etiquette messages (please, thank you, etc.). Many types of line drawing symbol sets are commercially available in a variety of sizes and forms (including some that permit a printed word on the card) from different companies. The symbols in these sets usually include those for people, places, activities, and items, as well as those for action verbs (eat, sit, sleep, etc.), feelings (happy, angry, bored, etc.), descriptors (hot, little, up/down, etc.), and social etiquette messages (please, thank you, etc.). The most commonly used line drawing symbols are called Picture Communication Symbols (PCS). A software program called Boardmaker™ is used by many people to produce communication displays of PCS symbols.

Alphabet Symbols

The last types of symbols we'll talk about here are alphabet symbols— A, B, C, D, and so forth. We use letters combined into printed words to represent many ideas and things every day—you're using these symbols right now in order to read this book! People with autism who know how to read can also use words and letters to communicate.

Even if a child doesn't know how to read *everything* he needs to communicate, words might be useful to communicate *some* things. For example, Jordan can recognize words for many foods he eats regularly, such as "Kellogg's Rice Krispies" and "peanut butter." He has several pages of these food words in a communication book that he carries around with him. When he wants to ask for something he likes to eat, he simply points to the word in his book.

The advantages of words are that many of them can be placed on a single page, and they are easily understood by people who can read. The disadvantage is that people with autism who cannot read will not be able to use them effectively. It is important to be able to distinguish between *word-calling*—when a child can name a written word—and *comprehension*—when a child can appropriately use a word or act on the word as equivalent to what it represents.

AAC Techniques

Now that you know about unaided and aided symbols, we can talk about what to *do* with those symbols and how they can be used to help a child communicate. Basically, two types of AAC techniques are available: nonelectronic or "low tech" and electronic or "high tech."

Nonelectronic ("Low Tech") Techniques

Nonelectronic or "low tech" techniques include:

- Communication books (for example, these may have cardboard or vinyl covers that permit some pictures to be shown on the cover while other pictures are stored within the book). Such books may contain symbols to point to or symbols that are attached (e.g., with Velcro™) and can be readily removed, as when using the PECS method described in Chapter 6.
- Communication boards on which pictures are either printed or affixed, and then covered with a clear laminate to protect the pictures from wear.
- Communication wallets (these may contain photographs or other symbols in clear plastic credit card holders).
- Fanny packs (for example, small pouches that can be strapped around the waist and that contain object symbols or other important items).
- Other devices that are neither battery-operated nor computer-based (such as date-books, notepads, Post-it notes, etc.).

Most of us use nonelectronic AAC techniques regularly, although we probably don't recognize it! Do you carry a "Daily Planner" to keep track of your appointments? Do you use a grocery list when you shop? Have you ever shared family photographs in your wallet with coworkers or neighbors, or pointed to a picture or foreign word in a menu to order your food in a restaurant? All of these are examples of nonelectronic techniques for communication!

As with all AAC techniques, there are both advantages and disadvantages to using "low tech" techniques for communication. The advantages are that they are relatively inexpensive; can be designed so they are easy to transport or carry around; and can be used in flexible, individualized ways. For example, one youngster had a few symbols of outside play equipment attached to a loop that hung on his belt so that he could use his hands freely on the equipment but also choose where he wanted to play next (e.g., on the swings, slide, etc.). The disadvantage is that someone must take responsibility for keeping these AAC systems updated with messages (symbols) that the child needs to communicate. Of course, this is also the case with electronic techniques.

Electronic ("High Tech") Techniques

Numerous *electronic or "high tech"* communication techniques that require some type of external power source (e.g., batteries or electricity) are also available. The primary advantage of electronic communication devices is that they produce output that can be readily understood by almost anyone your child might want to communicate with. Words might be displayed on a screen or printed out on paper, or the device might use voice output. For example, when a child touches a symbol on a voice output device, it "speaks" the message that has been programmed for the symbol.

Some "high tech" devices are quite complex and expensive, while others are relatively simple to program and operate. For example, the BIGmack (AbleNet, Inc.) is a small device with a built-in microswitch, which, when activated, plays a single recorded message up to 20 seconds long. Recording a message into the BIGmack takes only seconds, using the voice of whomever sets up the device. New messages can be recorded over old ones throughout the day. So, for example, with the assistance of an aide who is responsible for recording the messages, a kindergarten-aged student could use a BIGmack to:

a. greet his teacher and classmates on arrival at school ("Hi, how are you today?"), then to

b. recite the "Pledge of Allegiance" with his classmates, then to

c. participate in a language arts lesson by "reciting" the repeating line of a story the teacher is reading ("Brown bear, brown bear, what did you see?") and then to

d. call out "Duck, duck, duck, duck, goose!" while a classmate touches each child's head in the circle.

As you can see, the BIGmack might not do very much, but with some creativity and planning, it can be a very useful tool for classroom participation! Additional examples of basic electronic devices include the MessageMate (Words+, Inc.) and Talara (Zygo Industries, Inc.).

Other devices are capable of delivering more than twenty messages (in some cases, thousands!) and are more difficult both to program and use because they are more complex. Of course, the advantage of such devices is that they can contain a greater number of pre-programmed messages (e.g., "hello," "I need help," "I need a break," "I want to go to the bathroom," etc.). In addition, many of these devices have other features as well, including printers, calculators, large memory capacities for storing lengthy text and speeches, and the ability to interface with standard computers. Some examples include the ChatBox 40 (Prentke Romich Co.), Macaw (Zygo Industries, Inc.), and Dynavox Maestro (Dynavox Systems, Inc.). The vast majority of devices today use either digitized speech (i.e., human speech) or very high quality synthetic speech. The size of the buttons is not an issue since virtually all such modern devices allow you to customize the size of the target area to match the user's motor skills.

Aside from the cost (which can range from less than $200 to more than $10,000!), one of the major disadvantages of electronic devices is that they are more cumbersome and more vulnerable to simple wear and tear than are nonelectronic techniques. They can break down (which may require expert repair specialists); their batteries can run down or fail; the switches used to operate them can fail to function; a change in location can make it impractical to transport them; and they require someone to program messages into them on a regular basis. In addition, it is important to emphasize that having an electronic device does not make a person a good communicator any more than having a basketball makes someone Lebron James! Electronic devices are *tools* for communication, and children with autism will need to be taught how to use them in meaningful ways, just as they are taught to use other communication techniques. They should *not* be seen as "quick fix" solutions to the communication difficulties these children experience.

What about the iPad?

Since the release of Apple's iPad in 2010, professionals and parents have been exploring ways in which the tablet device might facilitate communication for individuals with a wide range of needs, including those with autism spectrum disorders (e.g., Kagohara et al., 2010). Since the iPod Touch was introduced in 2007, a number of applications, or "apps," have been developed. The iPod Touch has a small touch screen that can be difficult to manipulate without good pointing and other fine motor skills. However, the iPad has a nine-inch touch screen that is more accessible to individuals with varying motor abilities. The iPad, ranging in cost from $499 to $829 depending on the model, is also much less expensive than most current speech-

Table 5.1	iPod/iPad AAC Applications	
App	**Description**	**Price**
Answers: YesNo HD www.simplifiedtouch.com	Two-button speech generating app	$1.99
My Choice Board www.goodkarmaapplications.com	Speech generating choice boards	$9.99
I Can Speak http://lazyriver.on-rev.com/	Speech generating app	$29.99
Grace App http://graceappforautismoniphone.blogspot.com/	Nonspeech generating, PECS-based communication app	$37.99
Sounding Board www.ablenetinc.com	Speech generating app	$49.99
TouchChat HD www.silver-kite.com	Speech generating app	$149.99
Proloquo2Go http://proloquo2go.com	Dynamic display speech generating app	$189.99
DayLeaf www.friendleaf.me	Visual scheduling	$0.99
Picture Scheduler http://www.jankuj.com/Picture_Scheduler.html	Visual scheduling	$2.99
First Then Visual Schedule www.goodkarmaapplications.com	Visual scheduling	$9.99
iPrompts www.handholdadaptive.com	Visual scheduling, visual timer, choice making	$49.99

generating devices. Combined with AAC apps that range in price from $1.99 to $299.99, it is now possible to purchase a lightweight and powerful AAC "device" that talks for under $1000.

Several apps for the iPod Touch and the iPad can be used to support language understanding. There are apps to create visual schedules and Social Stories™, and there are even more apps to support expressive communication. These apps range from the simple to the complex. Some allow an individual to communicate a single message (e.g., *Tap-Speak Button*), some enable selection of one of a few messages (e.g., *Answers: Yes No HD, Sounding Board*), and some provide hundreds of messages (e.g., *TouchChat HD, Proloquo2Go*). Table 5.1 on the previous page lists some AAC apps and their prices. All of these apps, and many more, are available from the iTunes store (www.apple.com/itunes).

Designing an AAC System

Now that you have a basic understanding of the symbol and technique options that are available, we can consider some of the most important decisions that are needed to design an AAC system. These have to do with the types of symbols to be used and the types of messages that will be available for communication.

Symbol Selection

It's important to think carefully about what types of symbol to use with each child, because the same symbols are not necessarily best for everyone. The most important consideration is that the symbols should be easy for the child to learn how to use for communication. The more you know about a child's interactions with pictures and other symbols, the more likely it is that you will make a successful selection. For example, if a child spends time looking at pictures or photographs in books and magazines, then these types of symbols may be easy for the child to use within a communication system. If you lay out a group of symbols varying from color photographs to clip art to black-and-white line drawings and notice that the child primarily looks at and picks up the line drawings, then it may be helpful to start with such symbols.

Ultimately, the answer to the question "which type of symbol is best?" will only be answered by observing how readily a child learns to use symbols within a communication system. For example, in Chapter Six you will be introduced to PECS, a system for teaching communication skills to children with autism. Various types of symbols can be introduced through PECS, to see which one(s) the child learns to use most readily.

Messages

Perhaps the most important decision to be made involves the messages the child needs to communicate in various contexts. Communicative messages can be divided into four main categories, according to their functions: (a) wants and needs; (b) information sharing; (c) social closeness; and (d) social etiquette (Light, 1988).

Wants and needs messages are the easiest to learn how to communicate. Young children first communicate about wants and needs when they learn to say things like: "I want _____"; "Give me _____"; "No;" and "I don't want _____." Both nonelectronic and electronic communication devices should contain symbols that the child can use to make requests for food, activities, desired items, and people. There should also be symbols that allow the child to say "no," ask for a break, ask for help, and ask to be left alone.

Information sharing messages enable the child to share information with classmates, teachers, family members, and others. For example, most parents ask their children, "What did you do at school today?" when they come home after school. In addition, children often have a need to exchange more complicated information, such as when they want to ask or answer questions in class. Symbols that correspond to the vocabulary of the lesson (e.g., animals when talking about the zoo, symbols related to the holiday of the month, etc.) can help children share information and allow them to participate in these types of interactions.

Often, the purpose of communication is not to get what we want or to share information — it's simply to connect with other people and enjoy each other. Children with autism also need to be able to have such **social closeness** interactions. They need to be able to get the attention of others, interact in positive ways, and use humor to connect to other people. At least some of the symbols in their communication systems should be related to messages for social closeness (e.g., "Let's go play!" "That was great!" "I love you," etc.).

Finally, a fourth purpose of communication has to do with the routines for **social etiquette** that are important in specific cultures. In North America, for example, people are expected to say "please," "thank you," and "excuse me" in certain situations. It's also considered polite to say "hello" or "goodbye" when meeting or leaving someone and to shake someone's hand if it's offered. Students who use communication displays need to be provided with symbols that enable them to interact with others in ways that are culturally acceptable and respectful.

How can you determine exactly which messages from these four categories should be included on a display? Some questions to consider include:

- *Which messages will the child need to communicate on a regular basis (i.e., daily) or frequently (i.e., several times in a day)?* Some examples might include greetings, requests for help, "yes," "no," requests related to basic wants and needs (bathroom, water, food, etc.), and social etiquette messages (e.g., "please," "thank you").
- *Which messages will facilitate participation (e.g., information sharing) in family or school activities?* For example, a second grader might tell his mother what he did at school today by showing her "remnants" of various activities, such as paper scraps from his art project or the flyer he got at the school assembly.
- *Which messages will enable the child to participate in social interactions?* For example, a high school student at a pep rally might need a message in his BigMACK that says "Go, team, go!" Or, children of any age might want to talk about their family; fun events they did in the past; and favorite topics such as basketball stars or cars by using a scrapbook with photographs, cards, magazine pictures, and remnants that represent motivating topics.

You can see from these guidelines that most children will probably need to communicate dozens of messages each day! Initially, it is important to start by teaching the child to use symbols for the most motivating messages. However, it is important not to limit communication only to concrete "wants and needs" messages, such as *eat, drink, toilet, juice, cookie, puzzle,* and so forth. How boring! The communication system must be able to accommodate a sufficiently large number of messages to meet student's social, learning, and other needs as well.

Teaching Your Child to Use His AAC System

The first step in introducing an AAC system is for family members and all professionals to meet to discuss your child's current communication, motor, and learning skills and any specific deficits. This information will help in choosing and designing an appropriate AAC system. Each team member will make unique contributions to this decision based on his or her own knowledge of, and interactions with, your child. If your child is in a school-age, preschool, or early intervention program, this team should include the parents, the child, the teacher, the speech-language pathologist, other related-service providers, a psychologist and/or learning consultant, and an administrator.

Once your child's needs have been identified, the service agency will work with you, the parents, to identify what the agency will provide in order to meet these needs. The team members develop a plan for acquiring the necessary materials for introducing the communication system and for teaching the student to use it. Together, the team members create annual measurable goals and develop strategies that will be most effective in realizing those goals. If your child is in an early intervention program or considered to have a severe disability, the team also will develop measurable intermediate steps (benchmarks) that will help the team members to monitor progress throughout the next 6 months to a year. All of this information is included in your child's Individualized Education Program (IEP) or Individualized Family Service Plan (IFSP).

The following are some examples of annual goals and benchmarks:

Annual Goal: *Kim will request desired items from adults and peers.*

Benchmark 1: *Upon seeing a desired item, Kim will approach an adult and activate a single-picture message on her communication device at least 20 times per school day without prompting.*

Benchmark 2: *In a group art activity, Kim will ask a classmate for 2 items necessary for the project with no prompting during 3 of 3 art activities.*

The IEP and/or IFSP includes a description of who must do what, when, and where. In many cases, the speech-language pathologist will be the professional "in charge" of your child's AAC system. This means that she might be the person who introduces AAC to your child by determining which vocabulary to teach, teaching your child how and in what situations to access the vocabulary, etc. The speech-language pathologist also interacts with all other team members to insure that your child is using his AAC system as effectively as possible in all environments. Just as the "plan" for developing AAC should be created by a team approach, it should also be implemented as a team. For your child to become a successful communicator, it is imperative that everyone who interacts with him:

- knows how his AAC system works (e.g., how he turns on the electronic device and accesses the vocabulary, what his manual signs mean, or what the pictures he uses mean),
- expects him to communicate with them by creating situations in which communication will be necessary, and
- makes recommendations to the person "in charge" as to what additional steps must be taken to maximize the effectiveness of the AAC system. This includes ensuring that the student has the opportunity to interact with peers during a variety of activities.

Finally...

As you can see, there are many issues to consider when designing a communication system for a child with autism. You need to think about the types of symbols you will use, the messages that need to be conveyed, and many other factors. It can be overwhelming if you think that you have to "get it just right" from the very beginning. The truth is that even the most experienced communication system designers often need to experiment with various options before they find the best solution for a particular child. So, don't be discouraged, and remember—helping a child who cannot speak to communicate is probably *the* most valuable gift you can offer!

References & Resources

Note: Some of these publications were written for a professional audience. Those publications written for parents are identified with an asterisk (*).

Augmentative and Alternative Communication. Quarterly professional journal. Decker Publishing, Inc., One James St. South, P. O. Box 620, L. C. D. 1, Hamilton, Ontario L8N 3K7 CANADA.

Beukelman, D. & Mirenda, P. (2005). *Augmentative and Alternative Communication: Supporting Children and Adults with Complex Communication Needs.* 3rd ed. Baltimore: Paul H. Brookes.

*Bloomberg, K. & Johnson, H. (1991). *Communication without Speech.* Victoria, Australia: ACER.

*Cafiero, J.M. & Meyer, A. (2008). Your child with autism: When is augmentative and alternative communication an appropriate option? *The Exceptional Parent, 38(4),* 28-30.

*Cafiero, J.M. *Meaningful Exchanges for People with Autism: An Introduction to Augmentative & Alternative Communication.* Bethesda, MD: Woodbine House, 2005.

*Hill, K. & Romich, B. (1999). Choosing and using augmentative communication systems. Part 1: The goal, the team, and AAC rules of commitment. *The Exceptional Parent, 29 (10),* 76-80.

*Hill, K. & Romich, B. (1999). Choosing and using augmentative communication systems. Part 2: AAC success stories: Making the rules of commitment work. *The Exceptional Parent, 29 (11),* 60, 62, 64-67.

*Hill, K. & Romich, B. (1999). Choosing and using augmentative communication systems. Part 3: Assessment, intervention, and resources. *The Exceptional Parent, 29 (12),* 49-49.

Kagohara, D. M., van der Meer, L., Achmadi, D., Green, V.A., O'Reilly, M.F., Mulloy, A., Lancioni, G., Lang, R., & Sigafoos, J. (2010). Behavioral intervention promotes successful use of an iPod-based communication device by an adolescent with autism. *Clinical Case Studies, 9,* 328-338.

*McNairn, P. & Shioleno, C. (2000). Augmentative communication. Part 1: Can we talk? Parents' perspectives on augmentative and alternative communication. *The Exceptional Parent, 30(2),* 72-73, 77-78.

*McNairn, P. & Shioleno, C. (2000). Augmentative communication. Part 2: Can we talk? Parents' perspectives on AAC: Making sense of technology and making it work. *The Exceptional Parent, 30(3),* 80-83.

*McNairn, P. & Shioleno, C. (2000). Augmentative communication. Part 3: Can we talk? Parents' perspectives on AAC: Selecting the right system, now and as your child grows. *The Exceptional Parent, 30(4),* 74-78.

*McNairn, P. & Shioleno, C. (2000). Augmentative communication. Part 4: Can we talk? Individuals who use augmentative and alternative communication speak out. *The Exceptional Parent, 30(4)*, 74-78.

Millar, D.C. (2009). Effects of AAC on the natural speech development of individuals with autism spectrum disorders. In P. Mirenda & T. Iacono (Eds.) *Autism Spectrum Disorders and AAC* (pp. 171-192). Baltimore: Paul H. Brookes.

Millar, D.C., Light, J.C., & Schlosser, R.W. (2006). The impact of augmentative and alternative communication intervention on the speech production of individuals with developmental disabilities: A research review. *Journal of Speech, Language, and Hearing Research, 49*, 248-264.

Mirenda, P. & Iacono, T. (Eds.). (2009). *Autism Spectrum Disorders and AAC*. Baltimore: Paul H. Brookes.

*Murphy, P. (2007). Augmentative and alternative communication. *The Exceptional Parent, 37(8)*, 48-51.

Sennott, S. & Bowker, A. (2009). Autism, AAC, and Proloquo2Go. *Perspectives on Augmentative and Alternative Communication, 18*, 137-145.

*Weiss, M.J. & Harris, S.L. (2001). *Reaching Out, Joining In: Teaching Social Skills to Young Children with Autism*. Bethesda, MD: Woodbine House.

Technical Resources

AbleNet, Inc., 1081 Tenth Ave. N. E., Minneapolis, MN 55414-1312 (800-322-0956; www.ablenetinc.com).

Dynavox Systems, Inc., 2100 Wharton St., Pittsburgh, PA 15203 (888-697-7332; www.sentient-sys.com:80/000%20Index.folder/Home.html).

ISAAC (International Society for Augmentative and Alternative Communication), 49 The Donway West, Suite 308, Toronto, ON, M3C 3M9, Canada. (416- 385-0351; http://Isaac-online.org).

Mayer-Johnson Company, P. O. Box AD, Solana Beach, CA 92075-0838 (www.mayer-johnson.com).

Prentke Romich Company, 1022 Heyl Road, Wooster, Ohio 44691 (800-262-1933; www.prentrom.com).

Words+, Inc., 40015 Sierra Highway, Bldg. B-145, Palmdale, CA 93550 (800-869-2521; www.words-plus.com).

Zygo Industries, Inc., P. O. Box 1008, Portland, OR 97207 (800-234-6006; www.zygo-usa.com).

6 | The Picture Exchange Communication System (PECS): Initial Training

When I first met Sophie, she was three years old and had just been diagnosed with autism. She had no speech or formal communication skills. She clearly liked snacks and juice as evidenced by her taking chips and sips of orange juice when these were left on a table. When I held a chip in my hand, Sophie looked at the chip and reached for it. If I gently closed my fingers around the chip, she would pry my fingers open to get to the chip. Whenever she took things that I held, she looked at the item and never at my eyes. If I held the chip tightly, she began to cry. When Sophie saw a chip or a cup on a bookshelf too high for her to reach, she cried and fell to the floor. She also liked to watch a particular cartoon video. If the video were turned off, she did not turn to her parents or other adults but walked to the TV and began to cry and slap her head.

Everyone was concerned that Sophie's tantrums were increasing in number and severity. When we assessed her, we found that she did not imitate simple actions or repeat simple sounds or words. We taught her to use PECS whenever we noticed there was something that she wanted. Within a couple of days, she would pick up a picture, reach across a tabletop, and put it in the open hand of the person who held the item she wanted. Within a week, when the TV was turned off, Sophie would pick up a picture of her favorite videotape and give it to her mother sitting next to her. Everyone noticed how much calmer she now appeared and how much more time she spent interacting with her parents. At this point, she still was not a good imitator nor had she used any spoken words, but she clearly had mastered the first step in functional communication—she had found her audience!

Many young children with autism (i.e., those under five years of age) do not use speech or other forms of formal communication when they enter educational or treatment programs. When a child does not speak, of course our hope is for that child to learn to speak as quickly as possible. However, as we reviewed in our earlier chapter on functional communication, a critical problem for these children is that they lack communication skills in any modality. Furthermore, we also know that young children with autism often are very poor imitators of actions and speech, when they are first diagnosed. An important question is: Are there ways to rapidly help a child learn to communicate that do not require speech or imitation? Fortunately, the answer is "yes."

In this chapter, we describe the use of the Picture Exchange Communication System (PECS) in some detail. We developed this system (Bondy & Frost, 1994; Frost & Bondy, 2002) over a period of time, primarily with young children with autism. We provide details on how to begin the system and how best to develop more complex communication skills. In the next chapter, we explain how we teach more advanced lessons with PECS, including the use of attributes and learning to comment. Many of the training strategies described can and should be incorporated into teaching the use of any AAC system. Furthermore, some of the strategies described are highly effective for children with autism who are acquiring speech.

The Development of PECS

Over twenty years ago, we were working on communication skills with a young boy with autism who was not successful at vocal imitation or pointing to pictures. We had tried teaching him to point to a picture among an array of pictures that corresponded to things he liked. However, we encountered a number of problems with this approach. First, in part due to his young age, he had difficulty reliably using just one finger to touch one picture. In addition, sometimes when he touched a picture, his eyes were focused on something happening outside. We weren't sure if he really wanted what he was pointing to, if he wanted what he was looking at outside the window, or if he simply liked the sound of his finger tapping on the picture board.

We were also concerned about our observation that some children with autism had been taught to point to pictures when they wanted something but had not been taught to approach someone with the pictures to make sure that their message was "heard." That is, they could be sitting in the back of the room pointing to a picture on their board but unless someone happened to be looking at them, their pointing would be ineffective. They had learned to point to pictures, not to communicate—interact—with people.

Finally, we were concerned about the strategy traditionally used to teach children to point to pictures. That is, we had tried to teach children to match a picture with an object that we displayed. We would hold up an item, such as a ball, issue a simple instruction (using traditional though relatively odd phrases such as "match" or "find the same"), and teach the child to point to the corresponding picture. Many professionals advised that prior to teaching matching pictures to objects, we had to be sure that the child could match objects to objects. In each of these types of matching lessons, it was the teacher who started the interaction, not the child. Some children would only point to a picture when we began the sequence by holding up an item or using a spoken instruction. Therefore, these children were dependent upon prompts from adults to communicate and could not initiate an interaction.

Since the boy we were working with could not reliably imitate our actions, we had to devise a method to teach him to functionally communicate without imitating us. We thought this might be possible based on our knowledge that very young children typically learn to communicate independent of imitating others. That is, they learn to approach adults and engage in actions, which, though communicative, are not refined or formalized messages. (For example, an eighteen-month-old girl might look at her mother and simultaneously reach toward her ball that fell onto the floor.)

Given these concerns, we decided to teach this child to give us a single picture that corresponded to the item he currently desired. As with typical communication, giving us a picture required that he approach us. We started by making a line drawing of a pretzel, which was something we knew he enjoyed eating. With one of us enticing him with pretzels and the other one helping him with hand-over-hand guidance, we gradually taught him to give the single picture in exchange for the pretzel. Over time, we reduced the physical prompting and added pictures of other items and activities he desired to his "vocabulary." Eventually, we taught him to place several pictures in a row to construct a sentence.

We started using this same method to teach other young children with autism to communicate, and, in time, named our method the Picture Exchange Communication System (PECS). Our hope was that this method would accomplish several things:

1. The child would initiate the communication (rather than depend on a cue from the adult).
2. The child would find a communicative partner and approach that partner.
3. The child would use a single picture and avoid confusion that may accompany early discrimination between pictures.

We also hoped that this method of communication would avoid certain potential problems:

1. The child would not have to depend on prompts from the adult.
2. The child would not need to have learned to imitate actions or words prior to starting this lesson.
3. The child would not have to learn to make eye contact on demand prior to starting this lesson.
4. The child did not have to learn to quietly sit in a chair prior to starting this lesson.
5. The child would not have to master matching pictures to objects before quickly learning to communicate.

Of course, ultimately it is important for children to learn to imitate actions, sounds, and words, to sit attentively in a chair, and to look at someone on request. However, these are not prerequisites for a child to learn to functionally communicate her wants and desires. To functionally communicate, it is necessary for a child to approach someone and then deliver a message. And this is something that PECS most definitely enables many children (and adults) with autism to do.

What Are the Prerequisites for Starting PECS?

The primary factor to consider before beginning PECS is what your child does to indicate that something is reinforcing to her. That is, if she reaches for snacks, toys, trinkets, or other small items, then we are confident that we can teach her to reach for a picture instead of reaching for the item.

Your child does *not* need to have wonderful fine motor skills. If she has trouble picking up small items, the picture can be modified so that it is easier to manipulate. For example, the picture can be glued to a wooden or foam block or a dowel, to aid in picking it up. The size of the picture can be modified as well to help in manipulation.

The child does not have to know the meaning of the picture before starting PECS. Our aim in the first part of PECS is to teach the child to initiate an interaction with another person, so there is no reason to precede teaching the exchange by trying to teach the meaning of the picture. Not until the third phase of PECS training (covered later in this Chapter) do we focus on assuring that users select distinct messages.

We are not aware of any cognitive prerequisites indicated by scores on a standardized developmental test. That is, a child does not have to reach a minimum developmental age before she can successfully learn PECS. Instead, it is critical to observe that the child can clearly indicate (such as by reaching for a toy) what is reinforcing to her in a form that can ultimately be modified to manipulating a physical symbol, such as a picture. Again, skills such as eye-to-eye contact, sitting quietly in a chair, responding to a series of simple instructions, or matching pictures to objects or other pictures are *not* prerequisites for PECS.

Finally, a child does not have to be nonverbal to benefit from PECS. The primary focus during the first phase of PECS is on teaching communicative initiation. Therefore, while PECS is frequently used with children who have no spoken words, it has also been used effectively with children who say some words but do not initiate with those words.

Who Is an Appropriate Candidate for PECS?

We have found the following series of questions very useful in determining whether someone would be helped by PECS:

1. Is the person currently using functional communication?

 If "no"—then PECS is appropriate

 If "yes"—then PECS *may be* appropriate

2. Is the communication modality understandable to
   unfamiliar people?
   > If "no"—then PECS is appropriate
   > If "yes"—then PECS *may be* appropriate
3. Is the person initiating functional communication?
   > If "no"—then PECS is appropriate
   > If "yes"—then PECS *may be* appropriate
4. Can PECS help expand vocabulary or the mean-length/
   complexity of the message?
   > If "yes"—then PECS is appropriate.

What Are the Phases of Teaching PECS?

We've broken the sequence of steps to learn in PECS into six phases. In the first phase, children are taught to initiate communication. The second phase expands the use of pictures to other people, places, and rewards. In the third phase, making specific choices between pictures is addressed. The fourth phase teaches the child to construct simple sentences. At this point, we also begin to teach children to be more specific about what they want by teaching them how to use attributes to qualify their requests. The fifth phase assures that children can respond to the direct question, "What do you want?" while the sixth phase teaches children to comment about various items and activities.

This chapter covers Phases One through Four, and Chapter 7 continues with attributes as well as Phases Five and Six.

How to Begin Teaching PECS

Before we can begin to teach a child to communicate, there must be a reason for that child to communicate. In Chapter One, we noted two broad reasons to communicate: 1) to receive concrete objects, events, or actions; and 2) to receive social rewards, such as attention or praise. For very young children with autism, we have found that social rewards are not very effective motivators. Therefore, it will be more effective to teach communication about things that your child likes and that you can control access to.

Determining What Is Rewarding to Your Child

Before you can formally begin teaching PECS to your child, you need to determine what she likes—that is, to identify a number of potentially reinforcing items or rewards.

To do this type of reinforcer assessment, we must systematically observe what a child does. Note that there is no need to formally communicate with the child. While it would certainly be helpful to simply ask the child, "What do you like?" we can learn the answer by several other methods. First, we could ask the child's parents and other caregivers about the child's preferences. We can also carefully set up various situations and watch the child's actions. For example, we might simply hold a piece of candy in an open hand (or place it on a table) and observe whether or not the child takes the candy. We could also place several toys on a tabletop and observe which ones the child plays with (whether appropriately or in some unique fashion). We also observe what the child tends to spend a lot of time doing—we assume, for instance, that a child who stacks blocks over and over likes playing with blocks.

Ideally, we will find a set of items that the child likes. We also try to assure that not all of these items are types of food or drink. If all of her experiences involving PECS (or any other communication system) are linked only to snacks, then she will limit her use of communication skills to times when these snacks are available and not use them in other situations. In order for her to learn to use her new skill in a variety of settings, we must carefully plan to quickly introduce an array of opportunities to communicate.

Once we have determined which items a child likes, it is helpful to prioritize those items in a hierarchy. We do this by presenting the child with a choice between a pair of items. For example, we place a candy in one hand and a simple toy in our other hand, and observe which one the child reliably takes over a series of presentations. By pairing the candy with various items, we might determine that the child always selects candy as compared with other items. We next try this same type of comparison to determine the priority of other items offered to the child. We suggest continuing this prioritizing until you find items that the child clearly does not like—those she pushes away. Such items will be important when you want to teach the child to calmly reject some items or when you want to be certain of the child's choice between two items (e.g., "She likes candy but she hates pickles!").

During this preference assessment period, it is important to assess how much effort the child puts into obtaining whatever it is you are offering. It is unlikely that someone would work harder to communicate about something than they work to obtain the item directly. Therefore, if your child seems very passive or puts little energy into obtaining items, then we suggest first working on helping her indicate more definitely what she wants before you teach her to use PECS. Such effort may involve walking several feet to obtain something in view, prying open someone's fingers holding an item, or pushing aside a covering that is partially hiding a desired item. Essentially, if your child puts out little effort to obtain reinforcing items directly, she is not likely to put in more effort to obtain pictures corresponding to those items.

Sometimes when you are trying to figure out what is reinforcing for a child, it is helpful to look at what makes her protest. For example, your child may not actively approach the TV, but may watch if a cartoon-video is playing. Even more importantly, when you turn the TV off, she begins to whine and look around as if searching for what went wrong. Now is the time to begin a lesson because now she is most motivated to watch TV.

Phase One: Initiating Communication

The first step in PECS is to teach your child to initiate a request. Teaching strategies that require imitation or matching-to-sample as prerequisite skills often address spontaneous communication after children can imitate or respond to direct questions (such as, "What do you want?" or "What is this?"). We believe it is very important to teach children to be spontaneous communicators as quickly as possible, so initiation is the first goal of PECS.

Once you have found a powerful incentive as described above, introduce your child to PECS by teaching her to pick up and exchange a picture that corresponds to the item she wants. (See the sidebar on page 73 for information on making the picture.) First, you must ensure that your child will want the item when you are ready to begin teaching PECS. To increase the likelihood that she will, withhold the item from her for a period of time so that she comes to miss it. Then when you show her the item, she will be motivated to obtain it. Other strategies for enhancing your child's desire to gain access to an item are described in Table 6-1.

Table 6-1	Communication Enhancement Strategies*
1. Make favorite items inaccessible.	Place your child's favorite items out of reach but within view. Put the items on a high shelf, on a countertop, in clear containers with tight lids, etc. Don't automatically offer items.
2. Give small portions.	At meals or at snack time, offer bite-sized or small portions. Cut up a sandwich and give only part of it at a time. Put one or two swallows of a drink in a cup at a time. Help your child to understand that more is available by giving **subtle** cues such as saying "We have more juice," or by showing the food/drink item.
3. Consume a portion of a favorite food/drink in front of your child.	In view of your child, eat or drink a portion of the item she really wants. Show your extreme pleasure while consuming the item ("Boy is this JUICE good!!!")
4. Create the need for assistance.	Give your child access to a favorite item that he/she needs your assistance to enjoy. Encourage your child to seek assistance from you to wind the toy; turn on the TV, radio, tape recorder, computer, or something; open a container, etc.
5. Interrupt a favorite cooperative activity.	Begin a favorite activity that you and your child both participate in. Once you are both enjoying yourselves, stop the activity and encourage your child to signal to you that he/she wants to continue. For example, while pushing your child on the swing, stop her/him in mid-air.
6. Offer your child something that he/she does not like.	Offer your child a nonpreferred item/activity and encourage him/her to tell you "no" in an appropriate way.
7. Offer a choice.	Hold out two favorite items and say nothing. Expect the child to let you know which one he/she wants.

(continued on next page)

8. Violate your child's expectations.	Start putting together a puzzle with your child. After she has put in three or four pieces, give her a piece that obviously does not fit.
9. Surprise your child.	"Accidentally" spill, drop, or break something. Gasp and look at the "mess" and then at your child. Wait for a reaction.

*For a complete list of "Communicative Temptations," see: Wetherby, A.M. & Prizant, B.M. (1989). The expression of communicative intent: Assessment guidelines. *Seminars in Speech and Language, 10,* 77-91.

When using any of these strategies, once your child has initiated an interest in the item (looking at it, moving toward it, reaching for it, taking you to it), PAUSE and **WAIT. DO NOT** immediately prompt a response from your child (Do not ask "What do you want?" or say "Say, _____.") as this will likely result in imitation, direction following, or question responding. Waiting will enhance the likelihood that your child will spontaneously communicate with you!! Wait at least 5 seconds with an expectant look, raised shoulders, raised eyebrows, and then if your child has not responded, provide subtle prompts. These could include gesturing to his/her communication book, saying the initial sound of the word, or having a second person **MODEL** the response. Another technique is to say a "carrier phrase." For example, slowly say to your child "I want" and then pause expectantly after saying "want" and wait for your child to "fill in the blank."

When the first PECS lesson is started, your child's focus will be on the enticing item. How do we teach her to pick up the *picture* of the item? When we first tried this lesson, we tried the natural approach—the person who was holding the enticing item also physically assisted the child in picking up the picture and giving it to the person holding the item. We noticed several problems with this approach. One, if you hold an item up to the child and use your other hand to help guide the child to pick up the picture, you will be out of hands to receive the picture from the child! But more importantly, we found that if the person enticing was also the one helping, then the child tended to simply wait for the help. The solution involves having two people helping at this point in training.

One person is directly in front of the child and entices her with something desirable as described in Table 6.1. This person (whom we call the "communicative partner") uses no verbal prompts, thus avoiding simple questions or cues such as, "What do you want?" or "Give me the picture." These prompts tend to teach the child to wait for the question to be asked before responding. Furthermore, there is no reason to ask the question because we can interpret the child's reach as indicating what the child wants. When the child reaches for the enticing item, the second person, sitting or standing behind the child, guides the child to:

- pick up the picture (with whatever physical assistance is necessary),
- reach toward the first person, and
- place the picture in the open hand of the first person. The communicative partner immediately gives the child the item while saying the name of the item (see photo, next page).

For more detailed instructions about completing these steps, see "Designing Effective Phase I and Phase II Lessons" at the end of this chapter.

What Symbols Can Be Used with PECS?

As noted in the previous chapter, there are many symbols that can be incorporated into an alternative or augmentative communication system. We may use photographs, line drawings, product logos, or three-dimensional or miniaturized representations (such as kitchen magnets or actual items covered with resin). These symbols may be in black and white or color. Any of these types of symbols may be used in PECS as long as the child can easily manipulate them.

For some children, covering the picture with a laminate or contact paper will sufficiently protect the picture for repeated use and permit placement of material (such as Velcro™) to assist in attaching the symbol to a communication book. The backing of the symbol may need to be bolstered for some children. This support can be provided by thicker paper or cardboard, thin wood, plastic, or even metal (as from the lid of a frozen juice container). In situations when a child has physical difficulty in picking up or holding a picture, modifications of the symbol can be made via extensions (i.e., a wooden dowel attached to the symbol) or placing the symbol on a vertical vs. slanted board, providing a better angle for the child to grasp the symbol.

The role of the second person, the physical prompter, is (in this lesson) to reduce the physical assistance as quickly as possible. This reduction in help is best accomplished by using a strategy that at first glance seems backwards! That is, the physical prompter provides the child with physical help for picking up and reaching while eliminating assistance for letting go of the picture. Then, help is given for picking up the picture but eliminated (often in small increments over several opportunities) for reaching across to the open hand. This reduction in physical assistance can include changing the point of contact from the child's hand, to wrist, to elbow, etc. Finally, help is eliminated for picking up the picture. Formally, this strategy is called *backward-chaining.*

How quickly this help can be eliminated depends on a number of factors, including how motivated the child is to obtain the item and how skilled the physical prompter is at providing and reducing assistance. The physical prompter can be another professional, a relative, or even another child as long as he or she has demonstrated effective use of this teaching strategy.

Some children with autism have learned this first phase of PECS within a few minutes, while other children have taken several days. You should gear the length of your teaching sessions to your child's degree of motivation. You certainly do not want the lesson to run until she no longer wants the item you are using to entice her—otherwise, you would be trying to make your child ask for something she doesn't want! Therefore, it is difficult to predetermine exactly how many opportunities to insist on. We try to end the session while the child is being successful and still wants the item we are using, knowing we will set up other opportunities across the day.

A time will come when you do not want to give your child everything she asks for every time she asks! Maybe you have run out of the requested item, or it is not yet time for the requested activity. In any event, you will need to say "no" to your child sometimes. We will describe several different ways to handle this situation in Chapter 7.

Keeping the Rewards Rewarding

As mentioned above, your teaching will become ineffective if your child is no longer interested in the reward you are using to entice communication. It is therefore important to carefully choose rewards, as well as to make sure they remain rewarding.

Some potential rewards are quickly consumed. For example, snack items and drinks disappear once the child eats or drinks. In similar fashion, bubbles, stickers, wind-up toys, electronic devices (especially if you control the remote!), or tops also tend to disappear or stop working on their own. With these items, when a child has requested and consumed the item, she will most likely want another similar item. In general, it is helpful to start with such consumable items, as long as they are not all food or drink items.

On the other hand, there are some rewards that a child may keep. Such items include a favorite toy, doll, book, or similar material item. In this case, once the child has been given the item requested, how do we entice the child to make another request?

There are two strategies that can help. For some children, collecting more of their favorite item is still enticing. For example, a child who likes marbles may well be motivated to request other marbles from the teacher after she has been given one following her request. This way, she can accumulate many marbles.

The second strategy involves recovering the item by simply taking it from the child. In this case, we do not ask for the item, as that often involves a new lesson. Rather, we may say, "My turn" (merely to be polite) as we take the item back. If the child appears somewhat upset, another request is likely to follow as long as the physical prompter is ready to assist. Of course, if the child becomes so upset that she begins to severely tantrum, hurting herself or others, the lesson should stop. We advise using a more "consumable" item for this part of training until the child has learned to reliably exchange a picture for a desired item.

Phase Two: Expanding the Use of Pictures

The next step in PECS training involves introducing more realistic aspects of communication. For example, during the initial session, the communicative partner is positioned immediately in front of the child and all she has to do is extend her arm to reach her partner with the picture. Obviously, this arrangement is not typical of the real world. Therefore, the communicative partner must begin to gradually move away from the child in order to foster greater persistence on her part.

In a similar vein, the initial lesson begins with the picture immediately in front of the child. This arrangement, too, is not typical of the real world. In this case, we must begin to move the picture further from the child but still keep it in plain sight so that she will expend more effort to obtain the picture to bring to the teacher.

At this point in teaching, we introduce a *communication binder* for the child. This may be a three-ring binder that has a square of Velcro affixed to the middle of the front cover. A single picture used to communicate is displayed on the outside of this binder (placed there by the teacher), while other pictures can be stored within (see photo). The child's family or teacher makes sure that the appropriate picture is on the front of the book depending on the current activity or interests of the child. This binder will help the child identify her own set of pictures, as well as provide a location to place all the pictures she eventually may use.

During this second phase of PECS instruction, we expand the number of motivational items and activities. For example, if we used candy as the first reward in the PECS lesson, then we must introduce other items. In this case, it will be important to add items that are not similar to the first item—that is, something other than food. We may use a favorite toy or access to music or the TV. We must keep in mind that our goal is to teach the child how to initiate functional communication in all situations in which she desires something, rather than as the system used only during snack- or mealtime.

In summary, the goal of this second part of teaching PECS is to increase the:

1. distance from the child to the communicative partner,
2. distance from child to the pictures, and
3. number of items that the child can request.

These goals are accomplished while assuring that only one picture is placed on the front of the communication binder at a time.

Why are there no choices of pictures at this point in training? The key to the first part in PECS training is to teach the child to approach an adult in a situation in which there is something the child wants or needs. Recall that in typical language development, children learn to approach adults to communicate even before they have any formal message (i.e., words) to use. The goal in PECS is to achieve the same spontaneous approach even if the child has yet to learn to be selective about messages. Just as for children who acquire speech in the typical pattern, children learning PECS will learn to clarify their message after they have learned to communicatively approach someone.

Phase Three: Choosing the Message within PECS

Once children have learned the essence of communication—finding someone to communicate with—they then are ready to learn how to select specific messages. This involves learning to discriminate between pictures.

In teaching a child to discriminate between pictures, we need to individualize the teaching strategies as well as the type of symbols (i.e., photographs, line drawings, etc.) used. Although these issues are often entwined pragmatically, we will discuss teaching strategies before we describe message selection issues. Throughout the description of these teaching strategies, we will refer to the symbols as "pictures." Note: At this stage of PECS training, only one trainer will be needed, since the child initiates communication without physical assistance at this point.

Teaching Strategies for Message Selection

Life would be considerably simpler if there were one perfect teaching strategy to help children select from a choice of messages. In our experience, we have found instead that there are a number of helpful techniques to help children learn to discriminate between symbols. We will discuss some of the primary options, but strongly suggest readers look at the references provided at the end of the chapter for a more complete description of discrimination techniques.

During the first two phases of PECS training, children are presented with only one picture at a time. With only one picture to choose from, there is no way of knowing whether the child is connecting the symbol depicted with the item she is requesting. When we begin discrimination training, we place a second picture on the communication book in order to make sure the child understands how the pictures are related to specific items. To begin with, one picture will be associated with something that the child greatly prefers. There are several options for selecting the second picture (the distracter picture).

The distractor picture can be:

1. Associated with something that is either neutral or disliked or
2. Something that looks very different from the first item

Using Pictures of Neutral or Disliked Items as Distractors.
Using this option, you use a distractor picture of something that is either neutral (something boring such as a tissue, a piece of paper, etc.) or something that the child clearly doesn't like (pickles, lemons, etc.). We must determine which items are nonpreferred or disliked for each child. Their dislikes are as unique and individual as are their preferences. This strategy focuses on maximizing the difference in the value of each item for the child.

If we use this picture array (one picture of something preferred and the other picture of something nonpreferred or disliked), we give the child the corresponding item when she gives us a picture. For example, if the choice is between candy and a wooden spoon, when the child gives the candy picture, we provide candy; when the child gives the spoon picture, we give her the spoon. This strategy generally is successful if the child appears to be somewhat upset when handed the spoon. That is, if the child gave us the spoon picture and then pushed away the offered spoon, she is more likely to pay attention to the pictures to assure getting candy, and not the spoon. However, if the child calmly accepts the spoon and even begins to play with it, this strategy will not help the child be more careful in selecting pictures. In this case, choose another second item—something that the child is more likely to object to receiving!

Using Distinctly Different Pictures as Distractors. A second option in selecting the distractor picture is to choose something that looks very different from the first picture. For example, the second picture can be completely blank. Thus, the choice is between a picture of the item the child likes and a second picture that is simply white. This strategy maximizes the visual differences between the two pictures. There are several other ways to emphasize the visual differences between two pictures, including

    a. Color of item (e.g., one picture is black and white, and the other is in color)

    b. Color of background (e.g., the background of one picture is white and the background of the other picture is yellow)

    c. Size (e.g., one picture is very large and the other is very small) In each case, the distractor should be related to something your child does not prefer.

If we use this type of strategy, then we must quickly but gradually eliminate the prompt provided to help your child. For example, if your child can reliably select the regular picture when it is paired with a blank distractor, then you must make the blank card gradually more similar to other pictures. On the other hand, if you used differing colored backgrounds to help your child make selections, then you must gradually make those backgrounds the same. Whichever prompt you introduce to help your child make correct selections, you must gradually remove so that she learns to select pictures solely because of the contents of the pictures themselves.

Issues Associated with Successful Discrimination Training

Whichever discrimination training strategy is used, several broad issues must be systematically addressed:

1. how and when to provide feedback,
2. how to correct errors, and
3. how to make sure the child discriminates between two desired items.

Providing Feedback. In the first part of PECS, we wait until the child has given us the picture before we respond by providing whatever the child requested. However, in discrimination training, we now are focused on teaching the child to *select* the correct picture, since she has previously learned to hand us a single picture. Therefore, provid-

ing some vocal feedback (as in voicing "Oh!") or visual feedback (as in showing the desired item) at the point of picture selection will hasten the acquisition of this skill. This immediate feedback signals the child that she will soon receive the requested item. While we may respond vocally as the child selects a picture, we only provide the item when the student puts the picture into our hand.

Responding to Errors. Another general issue is how to react to the errors that children may make at this point in training. How should we respond to the child who rejects being handed the nonpreferred item? How should we respond to errors within a lesson?

The key is recognizing the difference between fixing the problem (which does not lead to new skills) and arranging to teach the appropriate response. For example, when we point to the right picture after the child has made an error, she is likely to pick up and give that picture, thus appearing to fix the problem. However, in this lesson, she is supposed to learn to select a picture from a pair of pictures, not take a picture pointed to by the teacher. It is important to respond to errors using a consistent strategy rather than simply repeat the sequence and risking repeating the errors. Remember, there is no one perfect way to teach discrimination, so you must be ready to systematically evaluate alternative strategies.

One strategy to correct errors within these types of discrete lessons—the *4-Step Error Correction Strategy*—involves taking time to go through a series of steps. For example, when shown a candy and a sock, if the child hands you the picture of a sock, and you are sure that she really doesn't want the sock, then:

1. Place both pictures back in their original position and show her the correct picture by pointing or tapping upon the candy picture.
2. Prompt her to practice giving you the candy picture (via holding your hand close to that picture, covering the other picture, etc.).
3. Provide praise for giving you the candy picture but do *not* give her the candy yet—after all, she is simply following your prompt at this point.
4. Repeat the first step by showing her both items. Now if she touches the candy picture, provide some feedback ("Oh!") and when she gives you the candy picture, give her some candy.

It is essential for teachers to be proficient at this strategy before trying any of the alternative discrimination strategies noted in the following section. In our experience, when children show difficulty in discrimination it is often because teachers are not using the most effective strategies, not that because there is a fundamental problem with the pictures being used. For more information about error correction strategies see *Autism 24/7: A Family Guide to Learning at Home and in the Community* (Bondy & Frost, 2008).

What To Do When Someone Does Not Look at the Pictures.
Sometimes people with autism reach for a picture—perhaps even the correct picture!—without looking at the picture. Even in the case of

a lucky guess, we should not reward reaching without looking. We suggest simply placing your hand on the picture and thus blocking this type of response.

If this strategy does not lead to more persistent looking before reaching, then hold up the binder with the picture choices at the user's eye level. If you hold the binder and picture just out of arm's reach, you should see when the child looks at the picture. Then immediately hold the book closer so that the child is rewarded with access to the picture when she looks at it. (Notice, this strategy is very hard to do if the book is flat upon the tabletop.) Once you see consistent looking before reaching, you may try slowly moving the binder in order to encourage improved tracking of the location of the picture, thus helping to promote visual scanning.

Discriminating Between Pictures of Two Desired Items. Once a child successfully selects from an array of two pictures, we gradually add more pictures. As more pictures are included, we begin to offer the child a choice between items that are more and more similar in preference. In time, the choice may be between two types of cookies or two types of chips. In such cases, how do we know what the child truly desires?

When we offer two equally preferred items, we seek to determine whether there is correspondence between what the child requests and what she wants. Therefore, in situations in which the child enjoys both (or many) of the items, we say, "OK, take it" when the child gives us a picture. Then we watch the child to be certain that she takes the item she requested. If she reaches for the chocolate cookie after giving us the vanilla cookie picture, then we assume an error was made. We also assume the child really wants the chocolate cookie (since that was the item she reached for), so we teach her to select the chocolate picture in order to take that type of cookie. Here, too, if an error is made, a systematic error correction strategy must be used.

Once a child can discriminate between two pictures, we present her with three, then four, then five pictures representing preferred items. We build an X-pattern with these pictures, rather than lining them up left to right. This strategy helps promote visual scanning in all directions. We periodically "check" the child's accuracy by having her "Go get" what she asked for. Eventually, the student learns to discriminate from among all pictures on the cover of and in her communication book.

Progressing to More Symbolic Pictures. Some people need to use three-dimensional or miniaturized representations or items

instead of pictures in the beginning of PECS training. As their reper-
toire grows, it is important to see if such symbols can be replaced by
less bulky two-dimensional representations. The following example
provides clarification on this point as well as suggesting the flexibility
we must provide to some children.

*Donna was eight years old and had successfully learned the first
steps of PECS. However, when her teacher and I began to work on discrimination, we encountered numerous problems. Finally, we found that
if we used three-dimensional items, discrimination was easier for her.
Over time, she gradually became successful at discriminating among
60 symbols. However, her communication book was now very large and
bulky, and Donna was having difficulty carrying it!*

*We began to place a small picture of the item on the lower left portion
of her three-dimensional symbols. At first, these pictures covered about 10
percent of the total surface of the object. Even this small change initially
resulted in a modest reduction of her discrimination accuracy, but that
soon recovered. At that point, we covered a somewhat larger portion of
the three-dimensional symbol with a slightly larger picture. Again, even
though the change looked minor to us, Donna's performance dropped
before once more recovering. Over the next few months, we continued
to cover her three-dimensional symbols with pictures until, finally, she
discriminated all of her symbols using pictures alone. As we added new
vocabulary, we generally first had to introduce the symbol with a three-
dimensional symbol before gradually replacing it with a picture. (See
Frost & Scholefield, 1996, for details.)*

Phase Four: Introducing Sentence Structure within PECS

*One day, my sixteen-month-old daughter came to me and said,
"Doggie!" while pointing to our dog running in the yard. Later that same*

day, she came over and again said, "Doggie?" but in a manner that led me to believe she was looking for her favorite stuffed animal. Even though she used the same word, she made it clear when she was commenting about something as opposed to when she wanted something. Her tone of voice, including inflection, prosody or rhythm, and other qualities of voice were the cues I used to better understand her message.

When children developing typical language are at a point in their use of words when they use only one word at a time, they alter how they say a word in order to help others understand their meaning. Early in the use of PECS, children use single pictures to make a request. However, in time, we hope to teach children to use communication to comment about things and events in their surroundings. How will we interpret a child's meaning if they only give us a single picture? Is there a way to teach children using PECS to indicate whether they are using a picture as a request or a comment? One solution is to teach them to form simple sentences to indicate either "I want ...." or "I see ...."

With our long-term goal in mind, we must introduce a new structure to help children use pictures to express different communicative purposes. Rather than try to teach a child a new structure and a new communicative function at the same time, we prefer to just add one new skill per lesson. Therefore, we will first teach a new language structure (sentence) and then teach a new function (commenting). (See the next chapter for information on teaching commenting.)

We introduce the new structure using the function that the child already uses—requesting. First, we design a Sentence Strip (see below) that can be readily removed from a communication book and on which pictures may be placed to construct a sentence. We design a picture with an icon representing "I want." (We do not use a separate icon for "I" and "want." At this stage, it is not possible to teach what "I" means because the child doesn't have any other pronoun in her picture vocabulary yet to contrast with "I").

We teach this lesson by starting with the "I want" picture already on the Sentence Strip, guiding the child to place the picture of what she wants on the Sentence Strip. The child is then guided to exchange the entire Sentence Strip. The child is then taught to place both the "I want" icon and the picture of what is desired onto the Sentence Strip before giving the strip to someone.

When we are handed the completed Sentence Strip, we encourage the child to touch each picture while we "read" the sentence to the child (i.e., "I want cookie."). While the child is learning where to place each picture and what to do with the entire Sentence Strip, we read the Sentence Strip quickly so as not to delay giving the requested item.

Once the sequence has become fluent, we introduce a pause between saying, "I want" and the name of the picture of the desired item. This pause tends to encourage children to initially imitate and often say the final spoken word before we do. Although we use this delay strategy to encourage and create opportunities for vocalization by the child, we do not insist on imitation, even for those children who may be speaking. That is, the expectation is on using PECS, not on making the child speak. Several people have reported to us that some children who are pressured to comply with vocal imitation within a PECS exchange begin to avoid using PECS as a way of avoiding the vocal imitation that they find difficult.

Designing Effective Phase I and II Lessons

Materials Needed:
Two or three powerful rewards. It may help to use rewards that are readily "consumable." For example, snacks, drinks, bubbles, spinning tops, music, or TV (where you control the remote!), etc. If you use toys, books, or other favorite objects, you will need to either have many of them or you will need to get the item back from the child to entice another communicative opportunity.

Pictures, photographs, product logos, or some other type of visual symbol associated with each reward. The pictures should be sturdy enough to handle frequently. Covering the picture with contact paper or lamination will help preserve the picture. The pictures should be about two inches by two inches. Avoid small pictures (pictures less than one inch by one inch) to begin with!

Prerequisites:
The child has been observed to seek out several powerful reinforcers.

People Needed:
Two teachers. One person entices with the reward (and gives the reward when a successful request is made) and the other teacher assists with physical prompting.

Physical Arrangement:
Begin with the child in between the two teachers, within arm's length of each teacher. The picture should be placed between the child and the teacher holding the reward.

The child does not have to be seated in a chair. Remember, we arrange this lesson wherever the most powerful rewards are found. Sometimes, that will be on the floor, in the sandbox, in front of the TV, or in some other interesting location. The teacher providing the physical assistance should be behind the child.

Starting the Lesson:
Scenario: John and Alexis are Sam's teachers.

*Sam likes raisins. John will entice Sam with the raisins, and Alexis will physically help Sam pick up, reach, and release the picture into John's hand. There is a picture of a raisin on the table where Sam is sitting. (Note: It is **not** necessary for Sam to sit to start this lesson—go where the reinforcer is!)*

1. At the start of the lesson, John holds up a raisin but does not say anything. Sam sees the raisin and reaches for it. John lets Sam have this raisin (using a "first one's free" strategy).
2. After Sam finishes that raisin, John holds up another raisin. Sam again reaches for it. Alexis immediately guides Sam's reaching hand to the picture, fully assists in helping him pick it up and place it into John's open hand (which John held open after he saw Sam reach for the raisin).
3. As soon as the picture touches John's hand, he says, "Raisin!" while immediately giving Sam the raisin.

4. Repeated trials are offered as long as it is apparent that Sam is still motivated to reach for the raisin. Over these trials, Alexis gradually reduces her physical assistance for the release, then the reach, and finally for the pick-up. Throughout the trials Alexis says nothing and is not involved in rewarding Sam for his actions.

5. As Sam begins to pick up the picture without assistance, John and Alexis switch roles. Alexis entices with the raisin and Sam immediately gives her the picture.

6. Training is now introduced during other highly motivating activities for Sam, such as for his favorite toy, a book he likes to look at, his choice of drinks (today it's orange juice but tomorrow it may be milk!), and related activities. These lessons also take place in various parts of the classroom as well as in different rooms at home. Opportunities to communicate are created throughout the day.

References & Resources

Bondy, A. & Frost, L. (1994). The Picture-Exchange Communication System. *Focus on Autistic Behavior 9*, 1-19.

Bondy, A. & Frost, L. (2008). Autism 24/7: A Family Guide to Learning at Home and in the Community. Bethesda, MD: Woodbine House.

Bondy, A. & Frost, L. (2009). Generalization issues pertaining to the Picture Exchange Communication System (PECS). In C. Whalen (Ed.), *Real Life, Real Progress for Children with Autism Spectrum Disorders: Strategies for Successful Generalization in Natural Environments.* Baltimore, MD: Paul Brookes Publishing Company.

Bondy, A. & Sulzer-Azaroff, B. (2002). *The Pyramid Approach to Education In Autism.* 2nd Edition. Newark, DE: Pyramid Educational Products, Inc.

Frost, L. & Bondy, A. (2002) *The Picture Exchange Communication System (PECS) Training Manual.* 2nd ed. Newark, DE: Pyramid Products, Inc.

Frost, L. & Scholefield, D. (May, 1996). Improving picture symbol discrimination skills within PECS through the use of three-dimensional objects and fading: A case study. Paper presented at the Association for Behavior Analysis. San Francisco, CA.

Sulzer-Azaroff, B., Hoffman, A., Horton, C., Bondy, A., & Frost, L. (2009). The Picture Exchange Communication System (PECS): What do the data say? *Focus on Autism, 24*, 89-103.

7 | Advanced Lessons within PECS

Sophie had learned to request her favorite candy, Skittles, using the Sentence Strip. Whenever we offered her a handful of Skittles, Sophie carefully inspected the choices and took only the red Skittles. If offered other colored Skittles, she pushed them aside. We realized that Sophie could select by color even though we had not yet used color within any lesson. The next time she requested a Skittle with her Sentence Strip, we said "Which one?" We provided a symbol for "red" on her PECS book and she quickly learned to form the sentence "I want…RED…Skittle." Soon, we found other objects for which color was important to Sophie and she used her new symbol whenever it helped clarify what she wanted.

Expanding Sentence Structure

There are two types of extensions to the use of the Sentence Strip introduced at the end of Chapter 6. One involves expanding on the type of request a child can produce by learning to use attributes such as color, size, shape, etc. The other involves the acquisition of new communication functions (i.e., learning to comment rather than request).

Phase Four (continued): Expanding Requests with Attributes

Once a child has learned how to use the Sentence Strip to make direct requests, we can teach him to clarify what he is requesting. As in the example with Sophie, first we noticed that particular colors of candy were important to her, so we taught her how to communicate her preference. We also began to design lessons in which color was made to be important. For example, we placed her favorite toy within a box that had a red cover and placed that box alongside a blue-covered box. To get access to her toy, she needed to request, "I want…RED…box." We designed additional "hiding" games to teach a variety of concepts.

Gary loved chocolate chip cookies and had learned to use a Sentence Strip to request them. We noticed that if we held a large cookie in one hand and a small piece of cookie in our other hand, Gary invariably reached for the larger piece. In this situation, Gary paid attention to issues related to size—he wanted the big cookie. We then created a symbol for "big" (i.e., a blob or splotch that fills most of the symbol area) and Gary learned to specify which piece of cookie he preferred.

In this example, Gary could choose appealing items by their size. However, while it may seem easy to get a child to ask for the larger cookie, how do we teach him to request things that are small? One way is to offer choices in which only the small item fits the situation. For example, if a child could request a spoon to eat pudding out of a small plastic container, giving the child a choice between a regular-sized spoon and the kitchen ladle would increase the appeal of the smaller spoon. Of course, to be certain the child was selecting by the relative size of the spoons, we would later need to offer a choice between the regular spoon and Barbie's spoon! Another approach to this lesson would be to hide a desired item in objects that varied by size. For example, we could put a piece of candy in a small plastic egg while placing tissue paper inside a large plastic egg.

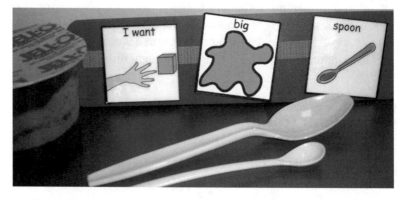

The vocabulary for other attributes, including number, positions, placement, and texture, can be introduced within the request function of PECS. (See Table 7-1.) Such lessons tend to be far more motivating to children than lessons involving understanding. Traditionally, attributes (sometimes referred to as "cognitive skills" or "conceptual vocabulary") have been taught to children with autism by placing in front of the student objects varying in the target attribute and telling the child to select by that attribute. For example, we would place a red circle and a blue circle before the child and say, "Touch red. Touch blue," or some similar

Table 7-1	Attributes
Type of Attribute	**Common Objects with Potential Motivators**
Color	Candy, crayons, blocks, Legos, clothes, juice, Skittles, jelly beans, Starburst
Size a) big vs. little b) long vs. short	Whole cookie vs. crumb, spoons that fit container Pretzel rods, string, "Fruit-by-the-Foot," licorice laces, bubble wands
Shape	Crackers, cookies, cookie cutters, form board puzzles
Location	Candy by the chair vs. candy by the table (one he likes, one he dislikes). For example, "I want... cookie...chair" meaning "I want the cookie on the chair, not the one that's on the floor"
Prepositions	Toy ON the chair vs. toy UNDER the chair (one he likes, one he dislikes). In this case, "on" is providing critical information about which item is desired.
Quantity	10 toy cars rather than 1 toy car
Temperature	Cold drink vs. hot drink, room temperature glitter wand vs. frozen glitter wand
Texture	Smooth cloth vs. rough cloth for back rubs, plain vs. salted pretzel, rough- vs. smooth-edged potato chips, lumpy vs. smooth cottage-cheese, smooth vs. textured ball, smooth vs. textured Tangle Toy
Cleanliness	Clean towel vs. dirty towel
Body Parts	Mr. Potato Head; placement of Band-Aids, stickers, lotion, ink stamps, temporary tattoos, brushing
Action words	"hit," "bounce," "throw," "catch" the ball

phrase. When the child correctly responded, we would then praise him, possibly providing an additional reward. Using the request function within PECS involves items that clearly are important to the child. The reward for successful requests is receiving the item the child specified.

Designing Effective Lessons Involving Attributes

Materials needed:

Items that vary only along the dimension associated with the attribute to be taught. (See the table above for examples of attributes and potential common objects.)

Prerequisites:

Before teaching a particular attribute within PECS, be sure that the child shows a preference associated with that attribute in terms of real items (not necessarily communicatively). For example, a child who selectively picks out red candies to eat, the blue crayon to draw with, or the white paper to draw on is demonstrating actions governed by color as an attribute dimension. In such cases, it will be very motivating to the child using PECS to request items with that specific feature.

It is very important to avoid confusing a child "knowing" or "responding to" an attribute with communicating about the attribute or understanding our attempts to communicate about that attribute. For example, we have met many teachers who were convinced that their student could not master "big" vs. "little." These teachers had done hours and hours of drills on "touch big" and "touch little" with various sized circles or squares, to no avail. However, with these same students, if I approached with a whole (big) cookie in one hand and a cookie crumb (little) in my other hand, I noticed that these students reliably took the big cookie and did not randomly respond (as long as they liked cookies!). The trick may be to separate the visual skill (or the skill associated with other senses such as touch, hearing, etc.) from the communicative skill associated with that sensory property.

If the child does not show a natural inclination to select by color, it may be possible to test his ability to visually discriminate by color without requiring communicative understanding. For example, assume that Lisa likes cookies. While she is watching, put a cookie inside an open, white-sided shoebox. You do not need to say, "Where is the cookie? Find the cookie. Look inside the box" or anything else. Just show her where you are placing the cookie. If she reliably reaches inside the box to take the cookie, then, over several trials, gradually place the lid on the shoebox. If, after you show her that you placed the cookie inside the shoebox and put the lid on top of the box, she reliably opens the box to get her cookie, you are ready to move to the next step. Now, you will want to have two shoeboxes: one with a red lid and the other with a blue lid. Show Lisa the cookie inside one box and place the red lid over that box and the blue lid over the empty box. Over trials, sometimes cover the cookie with the red lid and sometimes cover it with the blue lid, and be sure to move around the position of the lids. If Katie reliably finds her cookie, then she is showing us she 'knows' color. Next, we want to teach her to communicate about color.

Note: When using an attribute such as color, try to avoid using a symbol with a perfect circle filled with that color. In such cases, the child may be confused as to whether he should pay attention to the color or the shape of the color.

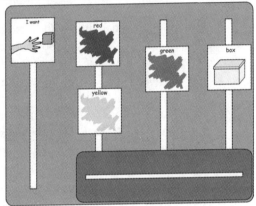

People needed:
One teacher can effectively teach this lesson.

Physical arrangement:
Have several pairs of items that vary only in the one attribute you are teaching. For example, if you are focusing on color, you will need pairs of items that are identical except for their color—candy, toy cars, crayons, etc. Although this

step will involve more time in preparation, it will ultimately pay off in reducing how long you will spend on teaching this lesson.

Starting the lesson:
Scenario: Marsha is Julie's mom.

*Julie likes Skittles (small fruit-flavored candies with brightly colored shells). Whenever Marsha offers Julie a handful of Skittles, Julie very carefully takes the red ones. Marsha will use this preference to design the lesson. (Note: It is **not** necessary for Julie to have learned to follow commands involving the word "red" ("Touch red") or for her to have mastered matching-to-sample with colors to begin this lesson. All that is necessary is for Julie to communicate her desire for Skittles using sentence structure (Phase IV in PECS) and her demonstrated preference for the red ones.)*

1. Marsha approaches Julie with a Sentence Strip containing "I want....Skittle." Marsha shows Julie two Skittles, one red and one blue. Julie reaches for the red skittle.

2. Marsha pulls back the Skittles (and she may shrug her shoulders, or say, "Which one?") and manually guides Julie to pick up a symbol for "red" on the front of the communication book. (Note that it is the physical guidance more than a spoken question that helps teach Julie what to do in this situation.) Marsha helps Julie place that symbol on the Sentence Strip between "I want" and "Skittle."

3. As Julie hands over the Sentence Strip, Marsha takes it, helps Julie touch each picture in order, while saying, "I want RED Skittle." Marsha immediately gives Julie the red Skittle. Of course, she does not try to make Julie say "red" or any other word.

4. Over the next several minutes, Marsha continues to entice Julie with Skittles and gradually reduces her manual assistance to guide Julie to use the "red" symbol within her Sentence Strip.

5. At other times, Marsha notices that Julie has her own way of building a stack of blocks. She seems to know precisely which block she wants next. Marsha holds onto a red block just as Julie is reaching for it. In this manner, Julie is encouraged to put together "I want...red...block" on her Sentence Strip.

6. Marsha continues to find situations in which Julie seems to have clear color choices and gradually introduces other color symbols into the communication system.

7. Finally, Marsha occasionally checks for correspondence with Julie. When Julie asks for a red crayon, Marsha holds up several crayons and simply says, "Go ahead, take it." If Julie takes the red crayon, then Marsha has another indication of Julie's level of skill regarding communicating about colors.

Phase Five: Teaching Answering Simple Questions

If your training in PECS has gone well until this part of the training sequence, your child should be requesting spontaneously using sentence structure and possibly attributes. In order to teach commenting, you also will need to ask your child simple questions about objects and events in the surroundings.

Since the PECS method teaches only one new skill at a time, you will need to introduce simple questions with the current communicative function used by your child, namely, requesting. At this point in the training sequence, your child has not heard the question, "What do you want?" Therefore, learning to respond to this question is our next step.

Teaching a child who can spontaneously request with a Sentence Strip is relatively easy. We simply need to ask the question "What do you want?" prior to presenting him with something desired. Over time, we would eliminate presenting items and solely ask the question. When we begin this lesson, it also is helpful to point to the "I want" picture while asking, "What do you want?" As quickly as possible over a series of opportunities, we would gradually introduce and then increase a delay between asking our question and pointing to "I want." In time, children come to respond to the question before the teacher points to the "I want" icon. Pairing your question with pointing to one picture in this lesson will prepare your child for the use of this strategy in our next lesson.

A word of caution is appropriate at this point. We have found that once parents and professionals begin to ask, "What do you want?" they have a tendency to rely on asking this question rather than continuing to emphasize spontaneous requests. Therefore, to preserve a blend of spontaneity and responding to questioning by others, you must plan to provide a minimum number of opportunities for spontaneous requesting each day.

Phase Six: Teaching Commenting

Once a child has learned to reply to "What do you want?" we are ready to teach him to respond to other simple questions, such as, "What do you see? What do you hear? What do you have?" To effectively teach these lessons, we must remember two points. First, we must remember that comments result in social consequences, not receiving the noted item. If we say, "What do you see?" and the child responds, "I see... spoon" we would respond, "Yes! It is a spoon! I see the spoon, too!" We would *not* give the child the spoon. If we did that, then the child would learn that this phrase is just another way to ask for something, such as "I'd like the spoon" or "Give me the spoon."

Second, we must understand the types of things and events that lead typically developing children to comment. Very young children do not comment about static aspects of their environment—they do not initially say, "I see the floor....I see the wall...." Instead, they first comment about things that change or are out of the ordinary. For example, they comment about the dog walking into the room, about the milk that just spilt, about a toy that is out of place, etc. Therefore, to design effective commenting lessons, we should strive to use similar types of interesting and eye-catching (or the equivalent of ear-catching, etc.) aspects of their surroundings. The more appealing the item used in the lesson, the more likely the child will notice that item.

We begin this lesson by suddenly changing something, such as taking a toy out of a box. As we take the item out, we ask, "Oh! What do you see?" or "Look! What is it?" While we ask our question, we point to an icon representing "I see" that has been placed on the communication book (on the left side on the cover of the communication binder). The child is likely to pick up the picture pointed to because that was a skill acquired in previous lessons. (Note: It may help to have only the "I see" icon on the cover for these initial commenting trials. Later, the child will learn to choose between "I want" and "I see.") The child may next place the appropriate picture on the Sentence Strip and hand it to the teacher. As before, the teacher reads the full sentence back to the child and enthusiastically praises him!

It may be very helpful to select items that are interesting but not your child's all-time favorite object. A child who has become used to receiving something concrete when he uses PECS may be surprised

(if not shocked!) when nothing concrete is forthcoming. This reaction would be more dramatic for items that were highly desired.

As your child learns this lesson, it is important to assure opportunities to request, both spontaneously and in response to direct questions. Therefore, your child will need to distinguish between the questions, "What do you want?" and "What do you see?" and their corresponding icons.

At this point, you must make one more change in your teaching strategy to promote spontaneous commenting. Essentially, you must eliminate your questions so that only the change or interesting aspect in the environment triggers a comment from your child. You may gradually eliminate the question, by leaving off the end of the question. For example, you could say, "Look! What do...?" gradually eliminating all words within your question. Finally, if you had been using exclamatory expressions such as, "Look! Wow! Oh!" preceding your direct question, then you could eliminate the question, leaving just the exclamation. Over time, you would then eliminate your expression as well.

What Comes After Phase Six?

Children who have completed each of the phases of PECS described in this book can: 1) request wanted and needed items

spontaneously and in response to questions, 2) comment about aspects of their world, again both spontaneously and in answer to questions, and 3) accomplish each function using various attributes and adjectives.

Of course, children also need to master other aspects to language development. Some of these, including social greetings, answering "yes" vs. "no," and requesting help, may involve some gestural skills, as previously noted. There is nothing incompatible about teaching these simple gestures while also teaching a child to use PECS. One emphasis is to teach with strategies that promote spontaneity rather than rely solely on imitation. For example, a child needs to ask for help before he has a tantrum over some frustrating circumstance. The teaching strategies for initiating asking for help or a break may require the same type of two-person teaching strategy used during the initial aspect of teaching PECS. See the example at the end of Chapter 4.

The teaching strategies and sequence of skill acquisition outlined for PECS also may be beneficial when teaching language skills with other modalities. That is, the techniques and decisions described for PECS—early focus on requesting, two-person prompting, delayed prompting, shaping, fading, formal error-correction, etc.—are not limited to using picture systems to communicate. These strategies can readily be incorporated into other types of communication systems, especially using two trainers to promote initiation.

Using PECS at School and at Home

The key to the success of PECS, or any other communication system, is for it to be used as often as possible. For this system to be effective, it cannot be scheduled for use "from 10:00 AM to 10:15 and from 2:00 PM to 2:15 PM," nor simply during snack time. This system must be viewed as the child's communication system, something that is potentially helpful in all situations. Limiting its use or limiting access to the communication book to when adults are ready to use it does not promote the development of spontaneous, functional communication.

Children who speak can do so at any time and in any situation. Therefore, you must assure that your child has access to his communication book at all times, although the vocabulary used at home may differ from that used at school. We see using PECS at home (if initially taught at school) as part of the second phase of training. You also should encourage your child to use the system with everyone in the home, not just you, the parents.

At School

When can children use PECS at school? We suggest that the school team (including the teacher, assistants, and the speech-language

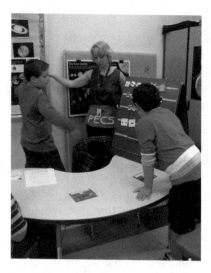

pathologist, and the parents at home) analyze all activities, noting the materials associated with each activity. For example, the art activity may involve paper, scissors, and crayons, while the circle time activity involves puppets associated with songs and sunny vs. cloudy pictures associated with the weather. Each of the materials is a potential source of communication.

Once your child has learned the routine associated with a particular activity, the teacher can interrupt or undermine the activity by removing a necessary item (Sulzer-Azaroff & Mayer, 1994). For example, your child may have learned to wash his hands and then use a towel to dry them. One day, if we remove the towel, we have created a situation that promotes asking for the missing towel to complete the sequence. Your child's school team should seek to find many such communicative opportunities throughout the teaching day as a way of expanding the use of PECS in the second phase of training. (More details on this strategy are reviewed in the next chapter.) In addition, it is important that school staff encourage your child to use PECS to communicate with peers, as described in the section below.

At Home

At home, we suggest a similar tactic. That is, consider the many natural routines that are available in a home environment, routines that will become part of the rest of your child's life. Examples include setting the table and routines associated with meal preparation and clean up. If your child has been taught to routinely set the table, then you can create a communicative opportunity by sabotaging the routine (with appropriate adjustments for the age of your child). For instance, you could remove all the forks from the drawer where they are usually kept. Some routines are uniquely related to the home situation and may be difficult to replicate at school.

Examples of home-based routines include:

1. Cleaning, folding, and putting away clothes (the latter can be viewed as a sorting or categorization task). For example, within these routines, a child can learn to request missing items.
2. Washing, showering, or bathing and associated objects (soap, towels, etc.) and toys (for the bathtub). For example, a child can learn to request needed items (e.g., soap) vs. desired items (e.g., the rubber ducky).
3. Unloading and sorting groceries (food or household supplies). In these situations, the child can learn to follow a schedule or to request necessary materials.
4. Cleaning and straightening the house.

Of course, we must keep age-appropriate goals in mind. For a three-year old, cleaning may involve putting away his toys, folding clothes may involve folding socks in half, setting the table may involve placing paper cups on each placemat, etc.

Each family may have their own special routines. We strongly recommend teaching and expecting children to participate in such routines. The following chart may be helpful in identifying potential vocabulary within common routines (feel free to add your own!):

Table 7-2	Finding Vocabulary within Routines	
Routine	**Area of House**	**Vocabulary**
Making cereal	Kitchen	Cereal, bowl, spoon, milk, sugar
Bath time	Bathroom	Bubble bath, washcloth, sponge, boats, bathtub stickers, toy duck
Going outside to play	House then back yard	Shoes, coat, hat, swing, ball, slide
Bedtime	Bedroom	Pillow, favorite blanket, book or specific books

Watching your child's preferences in the home is also crucial to developing increased communication. Some children enjoy watching TV or their favorite DVDs, while other children have their favorite songs. Some children have favorite toys or other household objects, while other children enjoy playing in the basement or the backyard. Your child can learn to request all of these activities spontaneously, and, as he acquires sentence structure, to clarify his requests with attributes and adjectives.

Using PECS with Peers and Siblings

I observed Michaela, a child with autism and skilled in PECS, who had been placed in a preschool class with typically developing children. As I observed, a small group of children, including Michaela, was playing appropriately with small, plastic figures. At first it was difficult to distinguish Michaela from her peers. Then, the other children became interested in toys in another area of the room and everyone left as a group—except for Michaela. She continued to play as before. One of the children from the group came back to encourage her to join them, but Michaela continued to play as before.

After further observations, it was clear that although Michela had skills to play with toys in an appropriate manner, she did not initiate, respond to, or maintain social interactions with the other children. If an adult in the class held a toy that she wanted, she immediately went to her communication book, constructed a complete sentence, and exchanged her request for the item. However, I never observed Michaela initiating communication or social interaction with her peers. I wondered how we would change this pattern.

So far, this books has focused on teaching the child with autism to use PECS with adults. We began by teaching PECS use with adults because typically it is adults who control access to the significant desires of a child. Adults generally control access to drinks and snacks, playthings, TV, computer, or DVD player, and visits to various places outside the class and home. It is not unusual to see children with autism acquire good communication skills with PECS (or speech or any other communication modality, for that matter) but limit its use to adults. How do we teach children like Michaela to communicate with their peers and siblings?

We know we must encourage contact between our children and their peers. However, we also know that mere exposure is not sufficient to result in significant improvements in communication or play with peers. (For more information on how to promote play see *Right from the Start: Behavioral Intervention for Young Children with Autism,* by

Sandra L. Harris and Mary Jane Weiss, Woodbine House, 2007.) We often have seen a communication progression involving peers that parallels the sequence observed when children with autism learn to communicate with adults. That is, children using PECS with adults will do so with other children initially to the extent that these other children have things that interest them.

Educators at the University of Washington developed a strategy that capitalizes on the tendency of children with autism to pursue things of interest to them (Schwartz, Garfinkle, & Bauer, 1998). They were aware that adults tend to control the distribution of drinks and edible treats at snack time. In their integrated preschool, they decided to give some of the snacks to the peers of several children who knew how to use PECS. At first, some of the children with autism continued requesting snacks from their teachers, but these requests were ignored. Most children quickly noticed that a peer now held their favorite snack. While some children needed some teacher assistance, others used PECS spontaneously with peers. Now came the tricky part—the peer had to be willing to share! This was encouraged by the teachers and richly praised when accomplished. Soon, the children with autism were communicating via PECS with both adults and their peers.

These educational researchers also looked at communication in other situations in which the teachers did not specifically encourage the use of PECS. Nonetheless, the children who had learned to communicate with peers during snack time now also communicated with them in these novel situations. Furthermore, the researchers also observed increased social approach and interaction (i.e., both initiating and responding to peers) in novel situations that did not involve any formal communication.

Drawing on this work and our own experience, we have developed some guidelines that make it relatively easy to teach children using PECS to communicate with their peers and siblings. The keys are threefold:

1. Distribute desired or needed objects to peers and siblings. For example, during an art activity, let classmates or siblings be responsible for distributing the crayons, paper, and other necessary materials.
2. Peers and siblings need to understand the content of the pictures and symbols used by the child using PECS. While age may limit successful responding to PECS, we

have observed effective interactions with children as young as two years old.

3. Peers and siblings need to respond to PECS just as they would to speech. That is, they should be encouraged and supported for sharing what was requested. Of course, with young peers and siblings, it may be easier to teach them to "share" things they are not thrilled with. For example, if Mary doesn't really like popcorn, she is more likely to give some to Bill than if he asked her for her favorite cookie.

Can children using PECS use their communication skills with other children with disabilities? As long as we keep the three issues noted above in mind, we have seen successful use of PECS within groups of children with various disabilities, including autism.

(Note: In the next chapter, we will discuss strategies that help peers better communicate with children using PECS or other communication modalities.)

What Is the Relationship between PECS and Speech Development?

Although this book is written primarily for an audience interested in individuals who do not speak, many members of that audience undoubtedly hope that these individuals will learn to speak. A reasonable concern is: will using an alternative communication system, such as PECS, interfere with or inhibit the potential acquisition of speech? As was noted in Chapter 5, there is no empirical, published evidence that introducing such a system will inhibit the development of speech. In fact, information that we have gathered regarding young children who learned PECS strongly suggests that the opposite happens. That is, use of PECS for more than one year by children with autism younger than six years is strongly associated with the acquisition of speech.

In 1994, we reviewed the communication modality for a number of children with autism who received educational services in a state-wide public school program (Bondy and Frost, 1994a). The program provided full-day, year-round services, had a high staff-to-child ratio, and provided highly structured, behaviorally oriented services, including the use of PECS when appropriate. We tracked the communicative progress of nineteen children who began using PECS before the age of six years but who had used the system for less than one year at the time of the assessment. Of these students, only two had acquired independent speech, while five other children were using speech primarily while they were using PECS. The other twelve students solely relied on PECS to functionally communicate. At the same time, we reviewed a group of 66 children who also had started using PECS at the same age as the other group but who had used the system for more than one year. Of this group, 41 demonstrated independent speech, while another 20 students used speech in conjunction with PECS.

Several points of caution should be made about this information. First, this information was retrospectively collected. That is, we had not randomly assigned students to receive PECS training or not. Thus, we have not demonstrated that learning PECS causes children to acquire speech. Furthermore, when we note "independent speech," we mean that speech was the sole communication modality of a child, not that the child had necessarily acquired age-appropriate language skills. Thus, while some children who had started PECS developed age-appropriate spoken language, others acquired a much more limited ability to use language. However, such follow-up information not only suggests that the use of PECS did not inhibit the development of speech but also may have contributed to its development.

More recently, there have been several thorough reviews of research regarding PECS. One (Tien, 2008) concluded, "PECS is recommended as an evidence-based intervention for enhancing functional communication skills of individuals with ASD (autism spectrum disorder)." Another (Tincani & Devis, 2010) noted that while there was initial concern that PECS might delay or inhibit speech development, review of several peer-reviewed studies found that "there is no evidence within the reviewed studies to suggest that PECS inhibited speech; to the contrary, if any effect was observed, it was facilitative rather than inhibitory." Finally, a third review (Sulzer-Azaroff et al., 2009) stated, "Findings suggest that PECS is providing people around the globe who have no or impaired speech with a functional means of communication."

Should PECS Be Abandoned Once a Child Begins to Speak?

A related question that often occurs following the introduction of PECS is: how should you respond to a child who may begin to speak after months, or even years, of silently using PECS? On hearing those first spoken words, both parents and professionals have the tendency to put the PECS book away and insist that the child only use speech to communicate. Our experience in such situations suggests a more cautious and gradual approach for reasons illustrated in the following two examples.

Jack was introduced to PECS when he was just about three years old. At the time, he rarely made any sounds. He quickly acquired the early skills associated with PECS. When he began to use the Sentence Strip, his teachers began to use the delayed read-back strategy. (They paused between reading back "I want" and the next picture on the Sentence Strip.) Jack then began to approximate some of the words in the sentence.

During the next several months, Jack's sentence structure became more complex and his ability to vocally imitate improved. Soon, his exchange of the Sentence Strip reliably led to his saying each word that corresponded with the pictures. Over the next few months, he occasionally would construct a sentence and then say the sentence without giving the strip to the teacher. He also began to say some words and simple phrases without using his communication book. Approximately twenty-four months after the introduction of PECS, he ceased using the system and used speech for all of his communication skills.

In Figure 1 you can follow the sequence of picture and spoken-word use by Jack after his introduction to PECS. He acquired his first PECS symbols during the first day of training. He rapidly progressed in acquiring additional pictures as he moved through the phases of training. We heard his first reliable speech-sounds after six months, while he spoke his first reliable word about twelve months after he entered the program.

Note that after Jack's first words were spoken, he did begin to speak more and more. However, during the months immediately following his first spoken word, his picture vocabulary increased by 50 percent. This growth involved new vocabulary, new syntax, and new communicative

Figure 1 | Jack's Vocabulary

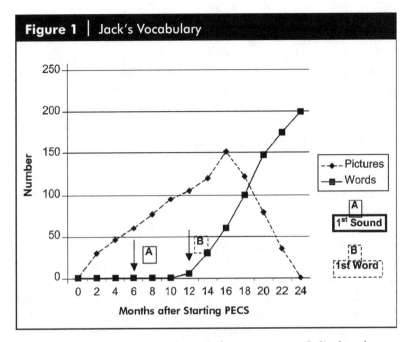

functions. For example, near the end of using PECS, Jack displayed some difficulty adding "-ing" to certain verbs (e.g., "He is walk-ing"). When an icon for "-ing" was added to his communication book, and he was taught to construct sentences with this icon, his speech production began to include the appropriate verb ending. What would have happened if we had pulled his communication book away at the point when his first words appeared? At that point, he could say or imitate single words but he could construct multi-element sentences with visual symbols.

Here is another example that illustrates why it pays not to be too hasting in weaning children from PECS once they have begun to speak. For several children who were using speech while continuing to use PECS, we arranged for comparable situations with and without access to their communication books (Frost, Daly, & Bondy, 1997). While these children used some limited speech when their communication systems were not available, their speech was significantly more sophisticated and comprehensive when their PECS books were accessible. For example, one child would say "cookie" or occasionally "I want" without PECS, but with her system, she put together a complete Sentence Strip and then said, "I want two green toys" or "I want big yellow candy." If had taken this child's PECS book away or tried to force her to communicate only via speech, she could not have communicated as well as she could using her visual communication system.

From our perspective, if someone were to suddenly take away a child's communication binder in an attempt to promote more speech, the resultant loss of skills (even in hopes of their replacement in the future) would be unethical. During a transition from one system to another, no skills should be lost. We can measure a child's skill in terms of the total number of pictures used as well as in terms of the complexity of the sentences the child can construct. We would also want to assure that if the child spoke, at least 70 percent of his words could be understood by a stranger before a visual back-up communication system should be removed.

Finally, remember that PECS is used to teach functional communication, not to teach speech. Of course, it is delightful when children do acquire speech and such changes should receive lots of reinforcement! For those children whose vocabulary continues to grow (e.g., over 120 or so pictures), switching to an electronic system may help promote continued vocabulary growth and ease picture selection (as noted in the chapter on AAC strategies).

Troubleshooting with PECS

The table on pages 111-112 lists the most frequent mistakes that teachers and parents make when implementing PECS. The table describes the most common mistakes within each phase and suggests straightforward solutions to these problems.

How to Say "NO!" and Live to Tell about It!

As soon as a child starts making effective requests for things, we adults face a complex choice. Should we always give the child what he requests?

Early in training of PECS or any other communication system, the initial requests are very important and everyone wants to be sure to reward those requests. Thus, if a girl asks for 100 pieces of pretzel on the first day of training, we give her 100 (very small!) pieces of pretzel because we are so excited with her new skill. However, after several

Table 7-3	Most Frequent Mistakes in Each Phase of PECS	
Phase	**Most Common Mistake**	**Potential Solution**
I. Initiation	1. No powerful reinforcer 2. Verbal prompting (e.g., "What do you want?" "Give me the picture.") 3. Physical prompting before reach	1. Find powerful reward 2. Practice silence 3. Wait for the reach
II. Persistence	1. One trainer 2. Only used at snack time	1. Wait for 2nd trainer 2. Create rewarding situations all day long
III. Choice making	1. Waiting to start (e.g., waiting for student to have 50 pictures before starting this phase) 2. Starting with too many pictures in the array (e.g., everything at snack time) 3. Waiting to praise until child gives the picture 4. Insisting on one type of symbol (e.g., all pictures *must* be black-and-white)	1. Start when 6 to 12 rewards are used 2. Start with one preferred and one nonpreferred 3. Give feedback on choice of symbol 4. Be flexible and try other strategies or symbols
IVa. Sentence structure	1. Waiting too long to start this phase 2. Verbally prompting 3. Insisting on speech	1. Start as soon as student has mastered array of 5 pictures 2. Not yet! Use physical prompts 3. Not now—not ever!
IVb. Attributes	1. Using only one attribute with one object 2. Insisting child complete matching-to-sample before starting this phase	1. Teach many qualifiers—color, shape, size, etc. 2. Start when the attribute is important to the child

(continued on next page)

V. Answering questions	1. Eliminating initiation (i.e., asking "What do you want?" every opportunity and thus undermining spontaneity)	1. Create, respond, and initiate opportunities
VI. Commenting	1. Boring materials 2. Predictable repetition	1. Materials should attract attention 2. Use surprise and change
VII. Transition from PECS to Speech	1. Insisting on speech imitation 2. Taking the pictures/PECS away from child 3. Rewarding only speech	1. Reward all successful functional communication 2. Let child set the pace 3. Bigger reward for speech

days, we are not as excited to give her what she asks for every single time she asks. So, what are our choices? We've held off on this question until now because the full range of responses available depends on many lessons. Here are some choices:

1. If the girl has eaten all the pretzels, show her the empty bag (and don't say, "no." Let her get angry at the bag rather than you!) Quickly offer her some alternatives. She is likely in this situation to "see" the futility of asking for more pretzels.

2. If it is simply not time for pretzels (or whatever her requested item or activity) then take the pretzel picture and put it on the schedule indicating when it will be time to have a snack.

3. Give her a "wait" card (see Chapter 8) and during the wait time entice her with alternatives that are available. At the end of the wait, see if she'll choose another item.

4. Show her a card with the available reinforcer menu and suggest she can choose from the menu.

5. If you have no available menu, you may want to place a universal NO (™) sign on the pretzel card, or place it on a board with a red vs. green side. The items on the green side are available, while those on the red side are not.

6. Consider whether is it worthwhile to negotiate with the child. Perhaps if she did something terrific (e.g., learned a

new skill, cleaned up her room, etc.) you would be willing to make a deal with her. In this case, use her request to start the token system described in the next chapter.

7. In the end, you may simply have to say, "no" and then watch the child have a tantrum. Of course, do make sure the child does not get hurt (or hurt others). Do not give in to the child at this point or tantrums will become (or stay) the primary mode of requesting. While the child is crying or otherwise being upset, show her—possibly with other children—what other rewards are available, and see if you can entice a different request.

Of course, the choice that many will want to take—simply taking the pretzel picture away from the child—is absolutely what you should never do! These are the child's pictures, part of his or her communication system. They are *not* the teacher's pictures or the parent's. Do speaking children ever nag us with their persistent requests and questions? Of course. While we might think of taping their mouths shut, we never do. And we similarly never take away the child's ability to use PECS to communicate with us. We may not agree or reward every request, but that is a natural part of growing up in any society.

Where to Go for Help

Hopefully, the suggestions above will help prevent problems or help you design successful modifications. Of course, you may run into unanticipated problems or simply have questions about how to apply the PECS system to your child. In such cases, there are several ways you may proceed.

First, it is important that a member of your team be competent in applied behavior analysis. The strategies described here have all been developed within this field, which focuses on the science of learning and, thus, teaching. The Association for Behavior Analysis International (www.abainternationa.org) can provide guidelines regarding identifying and evaluating the skills such as a specialist should have. Another broad resource regarding behavior analysis can be found on the website sponsored by The Cambridge Center for Behavioral Studies (www.behavior.org). The Autism Special Interest Group of this organization has written a set of guidelines that can help parents and others to identify skilled professionals in this field (*Guidelines for Consumers of Applied Behavior Analysis Services to Individuals with Autism*).

Second, a competent speech-language pathologist would also be an important member of your child's team. He or she can evaluate your child's communication abilities, both formally, with tests, and informally through observation; provide input about AAC methods; and advise parents and school staff about ways to incorporate language learning into your child's daily routine. In this area, the American Speech-Language-Hearing Association (www.ASHA.org) can supply appropriate guidelines regarding competency.

For additional guidance on the phases and associated teaching strategies of PECS, you can refer to our manual, *The Picture Exchange Communication System Training Manual*, 2nd edition (Frost and Bondy, 2002). There is also a DVD that provides a more visual overview regarding the system. These materials, as well as contact information for helpful organizations, are listed in the Resource Guide at the back of this book.

References & Resources

Frost, L., Daly, M., & Bondy, A. (April, 1997). Speech features with and without access to PECS for children with autism. Paper presented at COSAC. Long Beach, NJ.

Harris, S.L. & Weiss, M.J. (2007). *Right from the Start: Behavioral Intervention for Young Children with Autism*. 2nd ed. Bethesda: Woodbine House.

Schwartz, I., Garfinkle, A., & Bauer, J. (1998). The Picture Exchange Communication System: Communicative outcomes for young children with disabilities. *Topics in Early Childhood Special Education,* 10-15.

Sulzer-Azaroff, B., Hoffman, A., Horton, C., Bondy, A., & Frost, L. (2009). The Picture Exchange Communication System (PECS): What do the data say? *Focus on Autism, 24,* 89-103.

Tien, K-C. (2008). Effectiveness of the Picture Exchange Communication System as a functional communication intervention for individuals with autism spectrum disorders: A practice-based research synthesis. *Education and Training in Developmental Disabilities, 43,* 61-76.

Tincani, M. & Devis, K. (2010). Quantitative synthesis and component analysis of single-participant studies on the Picture Exchange Communication System. *Remediation and Special Education (Online First),* 1-13.

8 | Using Visual Strategies to Enhance Understanding

I worked with a teenager named Blanca. She never spoke but she effectively used PECS to request her favorite things. At times, Blanca would become extremely agitated and begin to slap her head with her hand. If you stood too close to her when she was agitated, she would try to slap you. We wondered whether she simply didn't want to do what we asked or whether she didn't always understand what was said to her. We arranged to give Blanca a set of simple spoken instructions about common items in the classroom. She retrieved only one of ten items and slapped her head following almost every instruction. We then used pictures to instruct her about the same set of items. When we used pictures, she not only retrieved all the items correctly but also did not hit her head during any instruction. Clearly, this pattern was more consistent with a comprehension problem than with a compliance problem.

The previous chapters have emphasized using systems designed to help children and adults improve their ability to communicate with us. That is, they have been concerned with improving *expressive* language skills. In this chapter, we will focus on ways of using visual systems to help these individuals better understand our attempts to communicate—in other words, to improve their *receptive* language skills.

Understanding Instructions

A skill essential to independence is understanding simple instructions, such as requests to get a common item, go to a location, or answer a direct question. In Chapter 2, we pointed out the importance of understanding things that are said to us as well as the importance of understanding various visual symbols. As in our example with Blanca, we also must remember that some individuals respond better to visual cues than to auditory cues. (A more complete description of this type of situation is presented in a study by Peterson, Bondy, Vincent, and Finnegan, 1996.)

There are many visual cues in our surroundings that help us function more effectively. They include:

1. **Personal**—day timers, calendars, clocks, Post-Its, notes to ourselves, shopping lists, Smart phones.
2. **Public**—road signs (including words, arrows, sign-post shapes and colors), restroom symbols, emergency signs, lines painted on the road, advertisements on public transportation, route numbers on busses or trains.

From this list, you can see that there are many visual symbols that everyone must learn in order to function effectively in our society. We believe it is important to teach children and adults who do not speak to understand these types of visual symbols as well. Traditionally, this type of lesson has been taught using a strategy called "matching-to-sample."

Many different materials and objects can be used during a matching lesson, but one important goal is for the child to select an item when we show her a representation of that item. For example, when I hold up a picture of a ball and the child gets a real ball, and when I show a picture of a cup and the child gets a real cup, then we conclude that she child understands what the pictures mean. Many teachers have simplified this type of lesson by having the child point to the corresponding item. In this case, we might have various objects on a tabletop and then show the child a series of pictures. When the child reliably touches the items that correspond to the pictures, then we say she has learned this task.

In addition to showing students pictures and expecting them to point to the corresponding items, we can also reverse the direction of this lesson. That is, we can hold up various objects and teach the child to point to the corresponding pictures. There is a fascinating field within behavior analysis (called *stimulus equivalence*) that has shown that learning this lesson in one direction (i.e., object to picture) actually eventually helps the child demonstrate the skill in the other direction (i.e., picture to object) even without explicit training.

Our question about such matching lessons is: can they be viewed as communicative? Such lessons are led by the teacher (the teacher holds up the initial object and the child points to the corresponding picture) and the response by the child is directed to the picture, not necessarily toward the teacher. This is why we suggest that such lessons should be part of a total educational package, but should not be viewed as a prerequisite to beginning lessons involving functional communication. In fact, when you introduce PECS to a child *before* you try to teach her picture-to-object lessons, such lessons may never be necessary. In other words, the child may learn picture-to-object correspondence in the course of learning to communicate with PECS.

Teaching Instruction Following

Throughout this book, our emphasis has been on teaching communication in a manner that is functional to the child—through lessons that involve objects and activities that are important and immediately a part of the child's everyday life. We need to continue this emphasis when teaching children to understand language.

Recall that one reason we learn to understand other people is that they often have information that is important to us. If we arrange a child's "listening" lessons so that she learns the importance of understanding what we are trying to communicate, we can enhance the effectiveness of the lesson. For example, you could try to teach your child to go to the couch, chair, or door on command. If she went where you requested, you might praise her. However, if your praise is not a reaction that your child likes and anticipates, she likely won't respond to many of these directions in the future once she realizes that she gets very little out of the task.

To make the direction-following lesson functional, hide something that is important to your child (some candy, a toy, etc.) on or near a particular item. For example, if your child used PECS to indicate she wanted candy, respond by communicating (in a simple manner) that the candy is on the couch. When your child gets to the couch, she finds the candy and is thus rewarded for having followed your direction.

A related approach is to have your child experience a pleasant, natural consequence when she goes to the couch, chair, or door when instructed. For example, the natural consequence of going to a door is getting to go outside, and the consequence of going to a couch to sit is getting to watch TV, etc. When using this strategy, it is important to tie the natural consequence into following the instruction.

Teaching a Child to Understand Pictures

When we begin to teach a child to understand the picture or symbol we will use within this instruction-following routine, it is important to make sure that the child understands the picture by itself. That is, while there may be times when we want to combine speech with visual cues, if a child responded to the combination, then we would not know for certain whether she reacted to the spoken words alone, the picture alone, or needed the combination of both for understanding. Given the need in our society to respond to visual cues in isolation from auditory cues, this lesson is important for all students. Thus, we suggest teaching the instructional use of visual cues without accompanying speech.

To start this type of lesson, we first make sure that the object to be used within the instruction-following lesson is very familiar to the child. The item should be one that the child either enjoys (like a ball) or one that she knows what to do with (e.g., put plates on the table before a meal). For example, let's assume we will use a picture of a bowl just before breakfast to signal to the child to get her bowl so we can serve breakfast. This picture would be a good choice for the child only if she has experienced that when bowls are on the table in the morning, cereal is about to be served! To begin the lesson, we would show the child a picture of the bowl and then quietly guide her to where the bowls are kept. The first few times we did this lesson, we would walk the child completely through the routine so there are no mistakes. Over time, we would start the lesson in the same manner, but then begin to let the child complete small portions of the end of the sequence. We would gradually reduce our help so that we would only need to show the child the picture and she would get the bowl and put it on the table and await her cereal.

At other times of the day, we would go through this same teaching strategy with other important materials (e.g., a ball to take to gym, a crayon to take to the art area, a book to join morning-circle, etc.). In this manner, we would try to build a set of pictures and/or visual symbols that the child associates with using materials in an understandable manner. We might also want to teach the child to respond to pictures or other visual cues that can be associated with specific areas (e.g., the art table) or activities (e.g., morning circle). To teach the child to understand spoken instructions, we could pair them either with the effective pictures or the functional items themselves.

Types of Symbols to Use

We've noted the importance of teaching all children to understand not only our spoken words, but also to understand various visual signals. What symbols should we select? If your child is using PECS, a good idea is to use the same type of symbols she is accustomed to within PECS. However, to avoid confusion, it may be helpful to use pictures your child understands but that are much larger than the ones used within the communication book (i.e., 4-inch squares instead of 2-inch squares). That is, your child exchanges 2-inch square pictures to request items but is given 4-inch square pictures by parents and teachers as part of an instructional interaction.

If your child is not using PECS, you may want to use any symbol that the child can understand—that is, photographs, product logos, miniature or full-sized items, three-dimensional representations, and similar symbols.

Instruction Following vs. Compliance Training

Finally, we should consider whether our goal is to teach *instruction following*, where the focus is on understanding the instruction, or *compliance training*, where the focus is on doing what we say (whether it fits the situation or not). For example, if we want to teach Mary to understand the instruction, "Go to the door," then we would be certain that something related to "doors" happens when she gets to the door (e.g., she gets to go outside). In similar fashion, instructions about the sink, refrigerator, a ball, etc. would all be connected with appropriate activities. On the other hand, if our point is to teach Mary to do what we say for the sake of compliance, then we could say, "Go to the door" and praise her when she gets there (but not have her go outside).

While there are times when compliance for its own sake will be important, it is not necessary to begin all instruction-following lessons with compliance as the focus. Furthermore, many young children with autism will not respond well to the social praise used in teaching compliance. In fact, some may learn to comply in order to avoid the physical prompts used when they do not do as they are asked.

Schedule Following

Most adults, especially those living hectic lives, use some sort of calendar system to keep track of important appointments and errands. We do this even if we have very good verbal skills. That is, even though I could probably make myself memorize all of the things I am supposed to do, I have learned that I act much more responsibly when I use various visual cues to help me remember what I am expected to accomplish. Furthermore, I intend to keep on using a schedule—that is, I don't think I'll be so much smarter next year that I won't need to rely upon such visual cues.

One of our teaching values is to teach children things that we have found to be important in our own lives. That is, if it's good for us, it's most likely good for the kids. Therefore, since we use a calendar system to help remind us about what is going to happen in our lives, we believe it is a good idea to teach children to use a similar system. Some children with autism may have fewer tantrums and other outbursts once they better understand the expectations for their time at school or at home.

Steps in Teaching Schedule Following

Teaching children and adults to follow a schedule is similar to teaching them to follow visual instructions. In fact, we prefer to start teaching children to follow a schedule after they have learned to respond to individual pictures. A schedule is a sequence of pictures or other symbols. What is important here is to teach your child to use the sequence of symbols rather than depending on a teacher or parent to tell her what to do. So, one simple rule is to avoid saying, "Go check your schedule." If you're willing to say that to your child, you may as well tell her what to do! Instead, teach your child to respond to natural cues in the environment, including:

1. The completion of a task (signaled by running out of materials or using all materials);
2. Sounds that signal the end of activities, either environmental (e.g., a bell, chime, alarms, etc.) or from people (e.g., the teacher says, "Music is over!");

3. Visual signals (e.g., classroom lights flickering, the teacher raising her hand, etc.);
4. Entering the classroom (such as at the start of the day or after lunch, gym, recess, etc.).

You can teach your child to respond to these cues using physical prompts that are faded as quickly as possible. For example, after your child puts her lunch in her cubby at the start of the day, a teacher/aide might physically prompt her to go to her schedule on the wall. Over time, the amount of help provided your child to go from the cubby to the schedule would be reduced. These teaching strategies are similar to what we described earlier—avoid additional verbal prompts, provide physical assistance preferably from behind your child, and provide positive outcomes that are as natural as possible.

We arrange the pictures and symbols on the schedule in a vertical sequence (in part because we start schedules with very young children, including those who may have difficulty with right-left discrimination). Another option is to include one activity per page in a separate booklet. See *Activity Schedules for Children with Autism: Teaching Independent Behavior*, 2nd edition (McClannahan and Krantz , 2010) for more details.

See the photo below for an example of an in-class schedule.

Understanding Changes in Routines and Expected Outcomes

Twelve-year-old Zena was terrific at using her daily picture schedule. She came into class each morning and immediately checked to see what her first activity was and whom she would be working with. However, her teacher found that there was one major problem. If something did not go EXACTLY as scheduled, Zena would get very upset and usually would not proceed with her schedule. While the teacher was happy that Zena had gained some independence, she was not pleased that Zena could not tolerate any change at all. It is one thing to try to perfectly control everything in the life of a three-year-old, but it is impossible to do so with a teenager. The teacher realized that no one had taught Zena to tolerate the changes that occur in all our lives.

Here we see an example of how learning one lesson—following a picture schedule—can sometimes create new behavior management concerns—intolerance for changes in the schedule. Therefore, it is important to teach such tolerance as part of the overall strategy for *all* students rather than waiting to see which students develop similar problems. There are several ways that such lessons can be arranged.

The changes that children with autism encounter tend to range from things they like (e.g., going outside to play, working with my favorite teacher, etc.) to things that are not as much fun (e.g., staying indoors because it is raining, working with a substitute teacher who doesn't know me, etc.).

One simple strategy for teaching a child to tolerate changes is to systematically introduce changes that are initially "good" surprises. For example, in schedules we design, we include a symbol that stands for "surprise"—this is often just a large question mark or the word "surprise" on a uniquely colored and shaped background. When the children first reach this point in their schedules, the teachers arrange for the "surprise" activity to involve lots of rewarding activities and treats. The "surprise" may be placed at any point in the schedule. At first, it often replaces work time or other less fun activities.

Over time, some of the "surprises" included in the children's schedules are activities that are less exciting. For example, surprises might include working with Ms. Jane instead of Ms. Marcia, or sitting in the back of the room for reading instead of in the front. Of course, we must make sure that such changes are not extremely difficult—at this level, they should only be mildly bothersome. Finally, the surprises tend to be work-related changes. For example, the surprise might be that computer time is coming before math time when it's usually the other way around.

We make sure that the students are richly rewarded for participating in these surprise activities. We want them to learn that the surprise picture might mean they have to do something that is immediately fun (e.g., party instead of work), or that the surprise activity will end in something wonderful just because they followed the schedule. It is important to maintain some "surprises" as highly interesting and motivating so that the children cannot predict which type of surprise comes next.

Once this mixture of "surprises" is part of the routine, when true surprises arise, the teacher can now simply put the "surprise" symbol on the schedule and assume that the children will be able to handle the change. Thus, our overall strategy is: "Since we all know that unexpected changes are part of life, why allow life to arrange for the lesson when teachers and parents can teach this lesson much more effectively?"

Understanding "Wait"

Mario was 19 years old and had for the past couple of years successfully worked at a job in the community. He seemed to enjoy his work, but what he enjoyed even more was going to get a hamburger at the end of each workday. Years earlier, Mario had displayed periodic episodes of extreme aggression but he had not attacked anyone for over a year. Mario's teacher routinely took him and another student on public transportation to their worksite as well as to their favorite hamburger location.

One winter's day, Mario's teacher was walking with both students when the other student sneezed. The teacher assessed the situation and quickly surmised that she would need to return to class and clean the student's coat. She knew there was still plenty of time to get on the bus.

The teacher signaled to both students that they needed to return to the classroom. She thought she had conveyed that the young men would need to wait for a moment before returning to their activity. The next thing she knew, however, Mario had head-butted her, nearly breaking a rib. He then started pounding her while she lay on the sidewalk. Why had he suddenly attacked her? Essentially, although she thought she had communicated for him to "wait," he thought she had communicated, "no, we are not going to get your favorite hamburger."

The long-term solution lay in developing a plan to teach Mario how to wait as well as to tolerate changes in expected routines. This type of training took over six months but at the end of this period, the teacher was able to request that Mario wait for an anticipated treat without any negative reaction.

Learning to wait can be a difficult lesson for many children. From one perspective, we can see that learning to wait is related to a child's self-control or the ability to calmly handle delayed gratification. However, we can also view learning to wait as a communication issue, since children need to understand what we mean when we say, "Wait!" For example, once a child has learned to request her favorite snack, eventually she will ask for the snack at a time when you do not have the snack with you. You are likely to say, "Wait! I'll go get it!" In such situations, it is important for the child to understand that "wait" is different than "no." When we say, "wait" to a child, we have essentially made a promise, as in "I know what you want and you will get it, but you will get it somewhat later than you expected." How can we teach this complex lesson to children who have significant communication limitations?

The key to teaching someone to wait for their expected reward is for the teacher to completely control access to the reward and the length of the waiting period. The need to control the duration of waiting from the beginning of training is the reason why it is difficult to teach this lesson in natural settings, such as at a fast food restaurant. In such places, we do not know how long anyone will need to wait for the food. It also is helpful if we know precisely what a child would like to receive after waiting for a short time. Therefore, this "wait" lesson is best started after a child has learned to reliably ask for the things she likes. Furthermore, we will use a visual cue to be associated with "wait" to make it more likely that the child will understand our message.

For example, if a child requests a cookie (over which we have complete control) with PECS, we can take her picture (or sentence strip) and immediately give her a visual symbol for "wait" (and, if we like, say, "You need to wait"). Because a symbol that is naturally associated with "wait" is difficult to represent, we make a large, brightly colored sign with the word "WAIT" boldly printed (see picture below). Whether the child actually reads the printed word or merely associates this unique symbol with "waiting" is not important at this point in training. While the child holds the wait card (undoubtedly wondering what is going on!) the teacher silently counts

to five seconds and then immediately says, "Nice waiting" while giving the child whatever was requested and taking back the wait card. Over the next set of trials, the teacher gradually increases the length of time for the child to wait. Generally, such increases should be done in small enough increments that the child hardly notices the change from trial to trial.

Of course, no matter how gradually you increase the waiting time, at some point your child is likely to protest! When this happens, it is important to prevent her from succeeding in obtaining what she wants through actions associated with protesting (e.g., crying, screaming, grabbing, etc.). Do not give her the desired item but wait for the protest to end. The next time, *decrease* the length of time your child needs to wait and then gradually lengthen the wait period over subsequent opportunities.

As with other objectives, it is important to incorporate general guidelines associated with the age of your child. For example, asking any child under five years old to wait for more than five minutes can be expected to elicit a tantrum regardless of her disability!

Another important part of this training strategy is to recognize some of your own adult preferences and to incorporate these into the training. For example, if you were in a situation in which you knew you'd have to wait for a substantial period of time (e.g., you have a doctor's appointment at 3:00 but you know for sure that you will *not* be seen at 3:00), you'd make sure you had something to do while waiting, that is, assuming you hate to wait and do nothing. You'd bring a book or something else to do, and if you forgot to bring something to read, there is always a magazine available—after all, the area where we wait is called "the waiting room!"

Therefore, as your lesson on waiting proceeds with your child, you should make certain that she too has something to do while waiting for what she really wants. Some of the options that you should have available and encourage use of include: playing with a simple toy, looking at a picture magazine, listening to music, etc. Remember, what your child is waiting for should be more important than what she is doing while waiting. The "waiting activity" should be interesting enough to occupy her attention but not so good that she doesn't want the item she is waiting for. For example, while waiting to draw on her iPad, she may doodle with a single crayon on a piece of paper.

Understanding Transitions

When Jaime arrived at school, she often was upset upon stepping off the bus, even before staff had a chance to say anything to her. On such days, she frequently cried while walking to class. Once Jaime was in the class, she generally calmed down after twenty or so minutes. Then the teacher would announce it was time for gym. Jaime would fall down and cry once more, and do so all the way to the gym. After twenty or so minutes in gym, she'd usually calm down. Shortly after that, the teacher would announce that it was time to go back to class. Once again, Jaime would start crying. During most of the transitions from one activity to another, she would cry and act out.

On the theory that perhaps Jaime didn't understand what she was being told, the teacher began showing her pictures of the next activity. That is, while in class, the teacher showed Jaime a picture of the gym and while in gym, the teacher showed her a picture of the class she would be returning to. This was mildly helpful, but Jaime continued to cry during most transitions.

Why did Jaime continue to have problems with transitions even after the teacher added a visual cue to her communications? Quite frankly, this step is often all that is needed to help children with autism make successful transitions. That is, as we have noted, some children do not understand our spoken words and the addition of visual cues helps them comprehend our message. However, Jaime seemed to need something more.

In addition to *how* we communicate, we must pay attention to *what* we communicate. In Jaime's case, the teacher chose to communicate about the activity change and the location of the activity, perhaps because this is the type of information we adults would include in our daily schedule system. However, we believe that many children with autism are focused on their reinforcers rather than their activities. If this interpretation is correct, then when we communicate to a child that she needs to change activities (by telling her about the next activity), the child remains focused on her immediate reinforcer. For example, notice that prior to each transition, Jaime was reasonably calm. She was likely engaged in some enjoyable action when the announcement came to change activities. If she were playing with crayons when she was told that it was time to go to gym, what Jaime understood was that it was time to give up the crayons. In similar fashion, when she had calmed down in gym to finally begin playing with a ball, she heard that it was time to go back to class. To Jaime, this message said, "It's time to give up the ball."

Whenever we have to give up a current reinforcer, we all act badly! Therefore, when we have a child such as Jaime who is focused on her reinforcers, then we should consider communicating about what she finds important. For example, while she is in the classroom, rather than communicating about the loss of the crayons, it would be more effective to communicate about the next reinforcer—in this case, about the ball that she enjoys in the gym. So, instead of announcing a change in activity, the teacher should approach Jaime and signal the availability of the ball, via pictures or the actual object if necessary. Such objects can be called "transitional objects." When she becomes focused on getting the ball, it can be calmly pointed out that we play with the ball in the gym. Thus, rather than highlighting what she has to give up, this strategy emphasizes what she can get next.

While Jaime is in the gym and playing with the ball, the teacher should approach her and communicate about the next reinforcer obtainable in the class—the crayons, snack time, music, etc. She will more readily give up the ball if she understands what she will gain by the change.

In situations where there may not be a natural reward related to an activity, it will be important to arrange for something positive to happen for the child once the activity is completed. This is the same principle that keeps many of us working at our jobs. That is, while we may enjoy some aspects of our jobs, we do other aspects because we know we are going to get paid. This same strategy is important to use with children who are learning lessons (see the next section for more details).

This strategy of preparing children for transitions by letting them know about reinforcers available works equally well at home. For example, we worked with one mother who liked to take her son for a walk after dinner. However, at some point, she would want to turn around and go home. When she would say, "Let's go home," her son would have a tantrum. Lengthening the walk would only postpone the inevitable screaming. When we advised the mother to communicate about her son's reinforcers rather than her scheduled activity, she decided to change her routine. Now when she goes for their walk, she has her son select a video (by taking the empty video cover) and she takes the cover on the walk. When she is ready to return, she simply takes out the video box. Her son knows that the VCR is at home and now leads the way back cheerfully!

Understanding and Using Visual Reinforcement Systems Or: Let's Make a Deal!

We all knew that Blanca loved to eat popcorn. Her teachers often used popcorn as a motivator to get Blanca to attend to and complete her work. However, the teachers noticed that Blanca often seemed unsure of when she could simply ask for or take some popcorn and when she had to earn some popcorn. The teachers also became concerned about how to communicate to Blanca just how much work she needed to do before having some popcorn. We asked her teachers how they knew how much work they needed to do before they got their paychecks, when they would get they pay, etc. They looked at us as if we were daft and said, "It's in our written contract!" We looked at them and simply said, "So?"

Blanca's teachers wanted her to understand that if she success-fully completed her lesson she would earn the popcorn that she liked. A great deal of communication is involved in this kind of arrangement—the teacher must know what the child likes, the child must know what the teacher expects, the child also must know how much work will result in how big a reward. Our point to her teachers was that when they make a "deal" with their boss, they insist on visual representation of that deal—a written contract. As we've noted earlier, one of our guiding principles is that "if it's good for us, it's good for the kids." Can we introduce "Let's make a deal" in an effective manner that will help Blanca and other children with autism become better students?

We can make a reasonable comparison between the teacher/ student relationship and the worker/boss relationship. First, let's remember that in our culture, students attend schools because they must. We have truancy laws to assure their attendance. When they show up at school, what is expected of them? Well, the most fundamental thing that teachers want of their students is for the students to learn.

What does it mean to learn? In its simplest sense, to learn means to change behavior. As teachers, we only know if our students learned a lesson if those students can do something differently after the lesson than they did before the lesson. Students can demonstrate their learning by saying something new—a new word, sentence, or idea, or by doing something differently—answering a question on a multiple choice test, tying their shoes, opening a container, etc.

So, when children come to school, they meet powerful adults who expect them to do something—to learn for the teacher. And who selects what will be learned? It is the teacher, with input from parents and the school system, who sets the curriculum. In what other relationships does a powerful person tell the less powerful individual what to do? One is in the parent-child relationship. Another is the worker-boss relationship, in which the boss wants the worker to do something—the job—for the boss.

How do we design an effective deal? We start by recognizing that our employer wants us to do something—the job. We only agree to do the job if we know what we will get in exchange for working. There are several important factors in arranging our "deal" with our boss. First, we would not accept the job if the boss said, "OK, I want you to do this job for a year and then I'll let you know what you will be paid." We would only accept the position if we knew our salary before we started to work. Notice also that we, not the boss, pick the type of reward for work (not how much—it's never enough!). We also want to know when we will get paid—weekly, monthly, etc.

Another critical aspect of our contract with our employer is specifying our benefits. One of the most important benefits is vacation time—my ability to tell my boss when I need some time off. Here, too, in typical contracts, we tell our employer when we will use our vacation days. Finally, as noted earlier, we insist that all aspects of our deal with our boss be put in writing—essentially providing a visual representation of our deal.

Teaching Children to Make a Deal

How can we design a system that will convey all of the same types of information that are in a typical contract between a worker and her employer to students who have limited communication skills?

Determine What the Child Wants to Work For. First, it is important to remember that we select our own rewards, and so too should the children. They can do so with PECS or other means. We can have them indicate their choices simply by offering them potentially rewarding items and observing what they reach for, or we can ask the child what she would like to work for, if she has the communication skills to reply.

Work First, Then Reward. We then teach the child about how we use "Let's make a deal." Once she has requested a reward, we indicate, often with gestures, for her to do something that is very simple—something that we know she can already do. For example, when your child gives you a picture of a cookie as a request, you might point and gesture to a toy on the floor, prompting her to give it to you. When she gives you the toy, you would immediately give her the cookie while saying, "Nice work!"

Gradually, as your child becomes more skilled at using PECS to make requests, you would begin to require small tasks to be completed prior to giving her what she requests. This interaction is your deal. Of course, you would not react to every request your child makes by starting a "deal!" In kind, it's important (and kind-hearted) to be certain to occasionally give your child things she likes simply out of love—no one should have to earn everything!

Introduce Reward Cards and Tokens. As the deals begin to require more work, there comes a point when your child may wonder what she is doing all this work for! At that point, you would put her picture icon on a separate card that states, "I am working for..." (or some similar phrase).

On this card is a single circle (usually containing a Velcro dot). Now, when your child completes the task you indicated, you immediately give her a token and show her how to place the token on the circle. This token is essentially the same as money that we are paid for doing our job. Since there is only one circle on the card, and it is filled with a token, the job is complete. Now you teach your child to "spend" her

token; that is, she gives the token to you and you immediately give her what she originally requested.

Just as every employer fundamentally wants "more work, same pay," teachers and parents also want students to do more work with less feedback over time—in other words, to become more independent. Therefore, when a child seems to understand the value of the single token, place a second circle on the work card. Now the child can only cash in the tokens when both circles are filled with tokens. Then, sticking with the tradition of requiring more work, gradually add a third, fourth, and eventually fifth circle to the work card. At any point during the deal, the work card contains information about: what the child can earn (i.e., the picture she used to make her request), how long the job lasts (e.g., it's a five-circle job), and how close she is to the next payday (depending on how many more circles need to be filled with tokens). It is important to start the system with just one circle—not the five that we hope to get to.

Taking a Break. We also may want to place a "break" symbol on the work-card to remind the child that she can request a "vacation" at any time. Teaching the use of a break-card is similar to how we teach Phase I in PECS. First, one person would place a demand on the child—for example, telling her repeatedly to stand and then sit. Before the child erupts in frustration, a second person (typically standing behind the child) helps the child hand the break-card to the adult placing the demand. This is the child's request for a break, which in this case means, "Please stop nagging me! I need a break!" Over time, the assistance is reduced until the child can independently request a break in similar demanding situations.

Once the child has asked for a break, we typically guide her to a quiet area, set a timer, and allow her to remain demand-free as long as

Designing a Contract

The questions below should help guide you through designing comprehensive deals:

Questions Complete Contracts Must Answer

- Who picks the type of reward?
- Who goes first? Remember to first determine the reward, before placing the demand.
- Can we renegotiate the deal?

The following elements must be visually signaled to the student:

- What am I working for? (Either the item itself or, when possible, a picture or other symbol that represents the item, such as a picture from a reward menu or the child's PECS book.)
- How much work is needed to get the reward? (The number of open circles on a token-card, the number of puzzle pieces a card is cut into, etc.)
- How often do I get paid? (Cash-in times—when the child gets to spend the tokens earned—can be noted on the child's schedule.)
- When is my next payday? (The child can tell by noting how many open circles are left on the token-card before completing this specific deal.)
- When can I take a break? (The "break" cards may even be placed on the reinforcer card.)
- What are the rules about my breaks?
  - How many do I get? (This is set by the number of break-cards made available.)
  - How long do they last? (Set a countdown timer—the child can set it too.)
  - What can I do while I'm on break? (What magazines or other low-reward items are available in the break-area?)

If possible, visually depict the type of work to be done (e.g., math lesson, putting toys away, setting the table, going to gym, etc.)

she stays in the break-area and for as long as we have set the time limit for the break. After the break, she should go back to the earlier task—after all, asking for a break is not the same as announcing, "I quit!"

It is important to determine in advance how often the child can request a break. One strategy is to think about your own vacations and the rules you and your boss agree to follow. Just as with our own vacations, there are rules about how long the break will last, how many can be requested within some period of time, and what we can do on break. Unlike a vacation—where we usually try to go someplace very rewarding—a break from work (or school work) is simply a request to get away from the demanding situation for a short while. Thus, while we would suggest having a break-area (certainly not the time-out area, if one is used!), we also suggest having only boring or mildly interesting things to do in that area. After all, we want to convince the child that it is more rewarding to complete the work than to sit in the break area!

As children mature, the deals stretch out and begin to resemble the typical adult work situation. We usually work for a couple of hours and then find some time to grab a snack, chew some gum, get a drink, etc. As students enter the workforce, they too will need to work for a couple of hours at a time before getting to the things they really like. Visual contracts such as described here help children with autism know what they are working for, how long they will have to work, and how soon the next reward time will come. While the system stretches over time, we never would totally eliminate it, just as we do not eliminate our contract with our boss even after years of employment.

Closing Remarks

Teaching children to be effective communicators is one of the most important and rewarding goals for professionals and parents alike. Everyone would like for our children to learn to speak in a comprehensive manner. However, as we have stressed throughout this book, children and adults who do not speak can still be excellent communicators. What these individuals need from us is patience to figure out what they want, skill to set up an effective training program, and flexibility to make thoughtful adjustments best suited to that person.

We hope that this book will spark your interest in following up on many of the resource materials noted at the end of each chapter.

The intent of this book is to provide you with assistance in making the first steps down a critical pathway. Our hope is that you will walk down that path hand in hand with the person you love or work with and let go of that hand when the time comes for independence. We hope you will find the many ways that our children can respond with expressions of their love for your efforts and dedication.

References & Resources

Bondy, A. & Frost, L. (2008). *Autism 24/7: A Family Guide to Learning at Home and in the Community.* Bethesda, MD: Woodbine House.

McClannahan, L. & Krantz, P. (2010). Activity Schedules for Children with Autism: Teaching Independent Behavior. 2nd ed. Bethesda, MD: Woodbine House.

Resources

PECS Training, Information, and Products

We (the authors) have formed a consulting group—Pyramid Educational Consultants, Inc.—to provide training and consultation regarding PECS and the Pyramid Approach to Education which incorporates various teaching strategies appropriate for children and adults with autism and other disabilities. Pyramid Educational Consultants provides workshops for professionals and parents designed to give people the necessary skills to implement PECS. We also have a PECS Certification process that allows us to identify people who have demonstrated skills in implementing PECS, as well as those who have demonstrated skills in supervising others in the use of PECS.

If a member of your child's team is providing your PECS support, you may want to check on the type of training they have received. We understand that some people with whom we have had no contact will be able to provide competent consultation regarding PECS; however, we can only comment about those who have completed our Certification process.

Pyramid also offers a range of products specifically designed to make PECS use and implementation more effective and efficient for children and teachers, as well as support for other visually mediated strategies. In addition, Pyramid offers a wide array of workshops for professionals and family members on many different topics. For questions regarding PECS or the Pyramid Approach, their use in programs, schools, or at home, please contact us at:

Pyramid Educational Consultants, Inc.
13 Garfield Way
Newark, DE 19713
888-PECS-INC (888-732-7482) Toll free within the USA
302-368-2515 (international calls)
www.pecsusa.com
Pyramid also offers services and products in at least 11 different countries around the world. For more information on which countries we operate in, please visit www.pecs.com.

Applied Behavior Analysis

Association for Behavior Analysis International
550 W. Centre Ave.
Portage, MI 49024
269-492-9310
mail@abainternational.org
www.abainternational.org

Association for Behavioral and Cognitive Therapies
305 7th Ave., 16th Floor
New York, NY 10001
212-647-1890
www.abct.org

Behavior Analyst Certification Board
2888 Remington Green Lane, Suite C
Tallahassee, FL 32308
850-765-0905
info@bacb.com
www.bacb.com

The Cambridge Center for Behavioral Studies
P.O. Box 7067
Cummings Center, Suite 340F
Beverly, MA 01915
978-369-CCBS (2227)
www.behavior.org

Autism and Communication Skills

American Speech-Language-Hearing Association (ASHA)
2200 Research Blvd.
Rockville, MD 20850
301-296-5700; 800-638-8255
www.asha.org

Autism Society of America
4349 East-West Highway, Ste. 350
Bethesda, MD 20814
301-657-0881; 800-3-AUTISM (328-8476)
www.autism-society.org

Index

Page numbers in *italics* indicate tables

About the Authors

Lori Frost, M.S., CCC-SLP, is a speech/language pathologist and co-founder of Pyramid Educational Consultants, Inc. She is co-author of the *PECS Training Manual, 2nd Edition* and *Autism 24/7.* Lori has taught international workshops and graduate courses on PECS, Verbal Behavior, and Functional Communication Training and consults to schools and families to create effective communication training protocols. She is co-creator of PECS, a unique system that allows learners with limited communication abilities to initiate communication with teachers, parents, and peers.

Andy Bondy, Ph.D., has over 40 years of experience working with children and adults with autism and related disabilities. For over a dozen years he served as the Statewide Director of a public school program for students with autism. With Lori Frost, he co-developed the Picture Exchange Communication System (PECS) as well as the Pyramid Approach to Education that combines broad-spectrum behavior analysis with an emphasis on functional communication. He is the co-founder of Pyramid Educational Consultants, Inc., an internationally based team of specialists from many fields working together to promote integration of the principles of applied behavior analysis within functional activities and an emphasis on developing functional communication skills independent of modality.